GREAT SCOTS
IN BUSINESS
the next generation

T E R R Y   H O U S T O N

B O O K S

Published in 1996 by Lang Syne Publishers Ltd, Glasgow, for Scottish Enterprise.

Printed by Dave Barr Print, Glasgow.

ISBN No. 1 85217 027 1

Contents

Foreword

THERE is no more exciting endeavour in the world than business. Not only are industry and commerce the life's blood of every nation, without which our very civilisations would crumble, they are also eternally challenging. The rewards from creating, running and growing your own company are considerable. Nor are they all monetary. Tap any successful businessman or woman on the shoulder and ask them why they are still filled with an enormous appetite for what they do, and they will all tell you the same thing: They enjoy it. They find business everlastingly fascinating. A lot of them will also add: "It's not about the money any more, you know. It's seeing how far forward I can take things."

They enjoy pitting their wits against the challenges they encounter. Business is like a never-ending chess game, filled with infinite permutations in response to changing conditions. Its horizons are limitless. There is probably no greater satisfaction around than taking the germ of an idea, developing it, putting it into practice - and seeing it work. The shopping malls we visit, the hotels and restaurants we dine in, the cars we drive, the clothes we wear - all these, and a million more everyday items, large and small, began life as a doodle or a scribbled financial calculation on someone's scratch pad. They are all someone's ideas and ambitions turned into a physical reality.

Today more and more Scots are discovering for themselves the joys - and the perils - of working for themselves in their own businesses. In part, that has been forced upon the country by the new commercial cycle the world has embarked upon. The shift in organisations has been away from massive manpower to smaller, multi-skilled core staffs. Computerised technology has fragmented the work scene as never before, giving rise to a wide network of independent operators servicing the larger companies. However, that is only part of the story. Abroad in Scotland today is a genuinely new spirit of enterprise and self-confidence. More new businesses than ever in our history are being set up.

That is why I welcome the arrival of this new book. The second in a series of books about Scottish business being commissioned by Scottish Enterprise, it is devoted to examining successful young businesses, how they get started, how they are being developed, and the background and motivation of their founders. That is valuable information, indeed. The early years of any new business are the definitive ones. The more mistakes young entrepreneurs avoid during them, the greater are their chances of taking those companies on to new heights. Within these pages, hopefully, many readers will find information relative to their lives, businesses (if they have them) and ambitions. For some it may alert them to early commercial pitfalls to be avoided, for others it may introduce them to unthought of new initiatives which can help their own businesses prosper. To any young people still teetering on the brink, thinking about starting a business of their own, it also offers enormous encouragement.

If there is a common theme running through the book's chapters, it is that a self-made business career is for anyone, whether they leave school at 16 or 17 years of age, as did Richard Emanuel and Craig Whyte, two of the fastest-growing young Scottish millionaires featured in these pages, or whether they go on to take an Honours degree at university. Irrespective of background, the young men and women featured here display to a quite conspicuous degree tenacity of purpose, resourcefulness, common sense and a hard-working optimism that they will achieve many of the goals that they have set for themselves. Fortunately for Scotland, there are thousands of such folk out there. This book focuses on just a few of them. In more than a few instances, the organisations they are building will go on to become important strands of the Scottish economy in the decades to come.

Two other thoughts strike me about this book. The comments in the last paragraph notwithstanding, it is heartening to note that the number of University graduates going into business for themselves appears to be on the rise. For a long time in Scotland, when it came to new business start-ups, graduates lagged behind nearly every other sector of the population. That "blip" seems to be righting itself, due no doubt to the country's increasing appetite for business and several fairly concerted long-term initiatives to encourage young graduates to step out on their own.

Equally pleasing is the large number of young people who, to get started, have sought out advice, help, training, grants or low-interest loans from the network of enabling agencies around in Scotland today. Though I say it, who perhaps shouldn't, the infra-structures which we now have in place in Scotland to aid businesses at all stages of their development are very much superior to that of many developed countries. In terms of support and back-up, we are now among the world's leading nations. That puts us in an excellent position to encourage and nurture the Scottish-based talent of the future.

But, as the man from IBM says, "Not a damn thing happens until somebody sells something." For that we are reliant on the young men and women in the book, and a lot of others like them. It's good to know there is so much talent and ambition out there.

Russel Griggs,
Business Development Director,
Scottish Enterprise.

May, 1996

CHAPTER ONE

Scotland's youngest self-made millionaire

AT the age of 15, schoolboy Craig Whyte quietly lifted the phone and for the first time spoke to a stockbroker. Using cash he had saved from his weekend job, the teenager was about to play the Stock Market, buying and selling traded options, a slightly esoteric futures market far beyond the ken of his schoolmates who were much more interested in their own youthful social scene than the financial world. Not realising the age of the confident-sounding young caller, the broking firm agreed to open an account with him. Soon it was handling regular transactions for its new client. By the time Craig left school at the age of 17, he had a larger bank balance than most of his teachers. Through shrewd stocks and shares manipulation, and the occasional reversal of fortune, he had amassed a sum in excess of £20,000. For Craig, it was the first step on the road to becoming Scotland's youngest self-made millionaire.

Today, at the age of 26, he is chief executive and owner of Vital Holdings plc, a conglomerate of companies providing a variety of services to the construction industry, retail stores and local authorities, ranging from heavy plant hire, security services and industrial and office cleaning. With an annual turn-over in excess of £12 million, annual profits of £1.5 million, and a total of nearly 750 staff on its books, the group in less than four years is already up

1

there among Scotland's top 500 companies. For Craig, it is only a beginning. He outlines his objectives extremely candidly: "I want to have a substantial and profitable world-wide business; I want to become a fully listed company on the Stock Exchange and one of its top listed companies; and I want to have major league personal wealth, which for me is over £100 million; and I want to achieve it all as quickly as possible."

He grins cheerily when asked why he wants such massive personal wealth, and says succinctly, "It's points in the game. It's just what you use to measure yourself against the Hansens, the Goldsmiths and the Bransons of this world."

He may be a young man in a hurry, but the last word anyone would dream of applying to him is brash. Although the enthusiasm for what he does bubbles through, there is none of the intensity which so often accompanies young chief executives; his is a fairly relaxed business style. He is also quiet-spoken, friendly, refreshingly normal and straight-forward, and quite without ostentation. The office in Wishart Street, Glasgow, from where he runs his fast-growing business empire, is entirely functional and bereft of executive toys. Even the 500SL Mercedes at the door is a muted black. To date, the rise and rise of Craig Whyte has been attended by remarkably little media publicity, although that is probably about to change as he steps up into the major league.

In that last respect, he is following a pattern. He has never been one to court the attention of his peers. At school, virtually no-one knew about his secret hobby. He never mentioned it to his friends; even his parents had little inkling of what he was doing with the cash which, whenever possible, he always took in lieu of birthday and Christmas presents. To all outward appearances, Craig was an ordinary teenager, enjoying the usual pursuits of a young man, with his circle of friends. The truth, though, was somewhat different. Craig Whyte was - and is - a self-taught Scottish business phenomenon.

To have a theoretical knowledge of the financial mechanisms which drive business is one thing; to confidently pull the levers of power, stitching together complex deals, loans and finance house accommodations with the aplomb and assured touch of an experienced financier, is quite another. Even by the standards of the eighties, and its helter skelter Stock Market boom, Craig's grasp of business principles has always been quite exceptional - as is his ability to actually put them into practice. Who among us, at the age of 19, would be capable of walking into the bank manager's office with £20,000 capital and a professionally prepared business plan to finance the start-up of our first company - and walk out with the pledge of a £60,000 loan? Not many. Yet not only did the teenager get the bank's backing, he also in the same week arranged deals with finance houses to acquire £500,000 worth of plant for his first business. That achievement takes more than courage and confidence; it requires a high degree of expertise in knowing how to use capital from one source to gain additional financial leverage from another. Craig knew how to make money work for him. From the outset, he understood its power, and was aware of how even a limited amount of capital could be used to drive a business forward, far in excess of the worth of the original sum.

Modestly, Craig says the climate of the times helped him; he doubts if it would be possible for a person of that age to do so today. The 1980s was a decade when the Stock Market - before its eventual "Black Wednesday" crash - kept climbing. Everyone was dabbling in the market, snapping up shares in the public utilities being sold off at bargain prices to the private sector by Mrs Thatcher's Government. To its critics, it was the era of the "get rich quick," grab all you can society, while Britain's manufacturing base was undergoing its severest contraction since the Hungry Thirties. To capitalists, the financial services industry was perceived as the new way forward for Britain. The market ruled supreme; there were fortunes to be won through the shuffling of stocks and shares and buying and selling on the money markets of the world. Very much a child of the eighties, Craig Whyte was capable of dealing and wheeling with the rest of them, although without the crass excesses of the high-flying yuppie dealers who were such a part of the London scene.

It would be unfair to say that Scotland's more staid financial institutions flung caution to the winds; but unquestionably their attitudes were coloured by the infectious, frenetic activity within the London Stock Exchange. However, it is too facile to explain away the ease with which Craig penetrated the business world by attributing it to that factor. The real truth is that the young entrepreneur impressed people with his grasp of the key elements of structuring businesses to give them the maximum chance of success. His expertise, despite his youth, shone through; and very often he was more alive to the important issues involved than those scrutinising and testing the soundness of his plans.

Brought up in Motherwell, Lanarkshire, with his sister, Adelle, Craig's background was one of comfortable affluence. It was also one where business was very much a way of life. His father, Tom, founded and ran his own successful plant hire company, first in Motherwell, then in Glasgow, before eventually selling out to another organisation 20 years down the line. His mother, Edna, owned a baby wear shop. "Business was all around us when we were growing up, and I obviously got very interested in ways of making money," recalls Craig.

Academically, Craig was a fairly average pupil. Unusually, his parents left

3

the choice of secondary school up to himself and his sister when the time came for them to move on from primary education. Craig plumped for the fee-paying Kelvinside Academy in Glasgow, for no other reason than a number of his friends were going there, while his sister later elected to attend the local Dalzell High School. Looking back on that time, he reckons he made the wrong choice. "I hated the discipline of it," he says. "It was a rugby only school, which I didn't play because I was interested in football. You also had to join one of the cadet organisations. I hated being told what to do; it was all terribly regimented. Actually, I didn't take it very seriously. I wasn't very academically minded. I was an average student, and picked up three Highers, but I only did what I had to do and no more. My parents wanted me to go on to university but I wasn't at all keen. I wanted work in my father's business, and he was absolutely OK about that."

In fact, Craig's over-riding passion at school, from third year onwards, was his discreet Stock Market speculation. Every weekend to earn pocket money he worked for his father's firm, donning over-alls to undertake manual tasks such as washing out machines or labouring to the fitters repairing plant. With the cash he saved, after studying the market, he began investing in traded options. A fairly high risk futures market, it offered generous returns to people with limited capital. In traded options, investors try to predict how much they think a company's shares value will rise over a set period of three, six or nine months. They invest in the right to purchase a tranche of shares at the end of the chosen period, paying a fixed price for them, which they hope will be lower than their actual achievement. If the shares perform well, the profits are considerable, often four or five times the original sum, which is well in excess of safer, but more conventional shares dealing. There is, of course, a down side. If the shares don't rise as expected within the valid period, the options simply expire, and the investor has nothing to show for his money. While at school, Craig was investing sums like £500 and £1,000 at a time, and steadily chasing up his bank balance.

"I'd read about traded options somewhere so I got some information from the Stock Exchange about the market, and decided it was an interesting way to make money," he says. "I also bought shares, particularly the big privatisation flotations. At my age it was probably totally illegal, but of course the broking firm had never met me. We only did business over the phone, so they had no idea I was still at school. I was quite good at it most of the time, but I did have losses. You can get too cocky and too smart. Black Wednesday, in particular, hit me. I'd left school by then, of course, and was working for my father. I'd just made a particularly good investment and decided to plough the lot back into the market when it collapsed. I lost a quite a few thousand, but that's what can happen."

The job in his father's firm was a lowly one. As a hire desk clerk, Craig answered the phone, took bookings, and handled breakdowns and replacements. He also dealt with sales from the company's retail division. Starting at the bottom may not have been glamorous, but it gave the teenager a thorough grounding in the nuts and bolts of the operation; it also put him in touch with a great number of clients, which was to stand him in good stead later on, when he set up his own company.

The decision to go into business for himself was actually forced upon him by his father's sale of the company to the BET Group, which was expanding into Scotland, and paying generously for suitable acquisitions. "My father probably got out at precisely the right time," says Craig.

The original deal was that Tom Whyte would stay on as part of the incoming executive team, under a new chief executive, Bob Tait, who had also sold his own Aberdeenshire-based plant hire company to the BET Group. The arrangement lasted precisely three days. In a clash of management styles, Tom Whyte's connection with the firm was severed. Caught in the cross-fire, Craig, although only a hire desk clerk, had to go, too. "I think the boss's precise words were, "I'd really prefer that you went, and I'll pay you for going," to which I replied, "That's for me," recalls Craig. "It was never going to work out and I certainly wouldn't have stayed for any length of time."

Following his departure, Craig took a couple of months out to consider his next move. Tallying up his assets, he realised three things: Construction work in Scotland was still booming; he had still a lot of contacts within the plant business; and he had built up excellent personal relationships with his former customers. On that basis, he decided to start up his own plant hire company, Whyte Hire, in McFarlane Street, near The Barras in Gallowgate, Glasgow.

He did it with some boldness of style, too. With complete self assurance, the teenage entrepreneur drew up a business plan to create a most substantial company, leaping into the hire market as a fairly major Scottish player - then got the financial backing for it. From his bank he obtained a £60,000 overdraft facility, then went on to bring finance houses and HP companies on board to finance the acquisition of £500,000 of construction plant. "I was totally confident," Craig recalls. "If someone had come up to me and said they'd give me £10 million I'd have spent that, no problem at all."

His confidence seemed fully justified. In the first two years of trading business was exceptionally good and everyone wanted to deal with the company. Having an enormously versatile range of plant available - eventually his purchases were to rise to £1.5 million - Craig's firm was able to supply, at speed, a lot of equipment which wasn't so readily available elsewhere. In its first year, the business grossed £770,000, making a profit of around £150,000, and performed similarly well in its second year.

During the third year of trading, however, things began to turn sour. In Scotland, the recession was beginning to bite and work for the construction industry - always among the first business sectors to feel the pinch - began to taper off. Whyte Hire found itself sitting with far too much plant. Even then, Craig would probably have weathered the downturn in business, but for another crushing blow. A blue chip construction company, which had been hiring a large percentage of the company's equipment, refused to pay a huge bill of £300,000. The dispute, which centred round claims and counter-claims about massive losses of equipment, blew a vast hole in the company finances; the debt was greater than the business's net worth. Gamely, Craig struggled on, but the task proved beyond him. For him the final humiliation came when the bank, which always had been tremendously supportive of him, failed to meet a wages cheque for his 20-strong staff. Craig put the business into voluntary liquidation, and it went down with debts of some £300,000. Later, when he started a new business, Craig was to rehire many of the staff, quite a few of whom still work for him today.

Looking back on that bleak episode, Craig says, "I regret it happening, but by the same token I learned an awful lot - a great deal more than you could ever learn going to university, which was what most of my friends were doing. These days, knowing what I do now, I'd have saved the company. Even with that major debt, and the fact that I'd bought too much plant and borrowed too much money, and the recession, I would have managed it."

Unusually, the company failure didn't dent Craig's confidence. "It hurt my pride more than anything else," he says. "For the first couple of years afterwards, I wouldn't tell anyone about it, I swept it under the carpet. Then I realised there's no point in doing that. I'm not the only person to have had a business failure. It's happened to a lot of people who have gone on to be extremely successful."

If proof were needed of Craig's continued self belief, deeds speak louder than words. Prior to going into liquidation he went round the finance houses and HP companies, telling them what was about to happen. "I offered every one of them a deal," he says. "I told them that if they didn't want to take the risk of losing money by repossessing the plant and selling it, then I would continue to honour the agreements if they rescheduled them over several years. Some of them did, some of them didn't. The ones that did ended up being paid in full. The ones who didn't lost their money."

Within weeks, Craig was back in business. He still owned another small, sole proprietor security business, trading under the UK Security Group name, which employed about 30 staff. He also founded another construction plant hire business, City Plant, buying some of the old equipment from the liquidator handling the closure of his old firm. His straight-forward treatment of the finance houses also worked to his advantage because those which had rescheduled his debts continued to support him. City Plant - which is still operational today, although now from Bellshill, Lanarkshire - was a much smaller version of his original business, with an initial annual turn-over of around £300,000.

However, Craig's attentions turned more and more to the security company. There were a number of reasons for this. In a very understandable reaction to past events, Craig was extremely wary of taking on company borrowings; he wanted to be involved in a business which did not require heavy capital start-up. Security service work was attractive because it was cash generative; you first landed the contracts, then hired the staff needed to fulfil them. It was a low risk venture. To the young tycoon, it also looked like a growth sector. Having done some research into the market, he realised that, against a background of steadily rising crime statistics, the "big boys" in the field were making a fortune. "It was a huge market and it was always going to be possible to get a share of it," he says. "The big factor, though, was that it could be grown without the same sort of capital expenditure on plant. There was a lot less risk. For a couple of years I was absolutely paranoid about taking on any sort of debt."

For 18 months, Craig gradually built up the two businesses, paying particular attention to expanding his security services. In that sector, the breakthrough came when the company began landing, with increasing frequency, contracts with Strathclyde Regional Council. Local authority work was a rapidly growing sector very much at the quality end of the market.

By now, Craig had also set out the company goals. Using his security company as the core business, his plan was to develop a range of companies servicing different aspects of the construction industry. Establishing that sort of base would create opportunities for cross-selling, and strengthen the organisation. He had also made a second decision, as instinctive as it was sound: Achievement of major growth would have to come through acquisitions.

It was a shrewd conclusion. Dotted across the country, nibbling at the market, were a large number of small, sole proprietor security businesses. On their own, they were never going to amount to a great deal. But if the key ones were pulled into Craig's business, they would make a considerable impact upon company growth. In late 1993, Craig put his reasoning to the test. He bought over Vital Security. Acquired for about £120,000, it brought with it about £1 million worth of contracts, boosting his turn-over from £2.5 million to £3.5 million. Jumping the business in size by a full one-third was an important development, but for Craig it was almost a side issue. "It showed me there was a quicker way to expand and move forward, and that these deals were abundant and fairly straight-forward to accomplish," he says. "It took me ages to put that first deal together because I wasn't sure if it was the right move to make. I spent three or four months on it; nowadays I would do the same size of deal in three or four days. I'm still very thorough, because I have a lot of good people round me, but on that first one I wanted to investigate every single detail myself."

In 1994 a succession of small companies were acquired, most of them being little more than the buying up of security contracts, and in some instances the debtors' book. However, the year did bring two very significant take-overs. The first, of a security company in Manchester, gained Vital Security a toehold in the English market for the first time; the second, of In Store Security and Property Protection Services, opened up a whole new avenue of retail security work, and also triggered off a number of retail sector contracts which were in place, including a major one with Kwik-Save. Other big contracts In Store has are with HMV, Superdrug and Asda.

In that year, too, he acquired his first overseas company, purchasing a 75 per cent stake in the Vietnam Trading Company which, from a factory base in Hanoi, manufactures fire-proof gypsum ceiling tiles for sale in Singapore and Hong Kong, as well as in Vietnam. With a workforce of about 40, it also has a sales office in Ho Chi Minh City. The unusual acquisition arose from a "busman's holiday" Craig went on to the Far East. He says, "A friend of mine from the Isle of Wight had business interests out there, and I went out to see for myself. It's what I do instead of holidays. Foreign nationals are allowed to buy businesses provided they also have a Vietnamese partner, so I bought the principal stake in the company and expanded it. I go out there a couple of times a year. It's a beautiful country."

However, it was Craig's UK acquisitions that year which mattered most. They were important building bricks, laying the foundations for further expansion in 1995, which began with another acquisition in England of Cathedral Security, a company in Durham. In April of that year Craig also started up a brand new company, Custom Cleaning Services. Its role was to handle office cleaning, special contracts and industrial cleaning - all part of Craig's strategy of creating a series of linked industrial service businesses fitting in with his client base. In support of that goal, in August of that year, he acquired another company, Hire Access, which took him, for the first time, into aluminium scaffolding hire. In December, the young businessman clinched his biggest deal of all, taking over the Plant and Transport division of Hall & Tawse Scotland, a highly respected construction business which is part of the Raines Group, to allow it to concentrate on its core activities.

It was a considerable business coup. To acquire the division, Craig beat off several predators, paying £750,000 for it, while also negotiating a deal worth £7.5 million to lease back equipment to the company over a three-year period. Also flung into the pot were arrangements to provide Hall & Tawse with site security and contract cleaning services in Aberdeen, Glasgow, Dundee and Edinburgh. The deal went through under his new company, Vital Holdings plc, which was set up specifically to bring all the various strands of his businesses together under the one umbrella. As well as obtaining one of the largest, and best maintained plant fleets in Scotland (some 2,000 items of equipment, ranging from 45-tonne cranes to excavators, were added to his plant hire business division) the deal also gave him access to a new geographic span of plant hire depots covering Aberdeen, Elgin, Glasgow and Broxburn, and this year, also Dundee and Newcastle. That depth of depot cover is an extremely important stepping stone towards further expansion through the development of new hire markets. All in all, Craig had every reason to feel well satisfied with the deal. In one swoop, he transformed his plant hire division from a medium-sized business into a major Scottish player, and also laid down the infra-structure for further growth.

Needless to say, it was not a negotiation which was concluded in his customary four days. It took several months to put together. However, for anyone thinking of treading the acquisition trail, Craig's methodology for smaller deals is straight-forward. Having satisfied himself of the worth of the business, and having thoroughly checked its assets, the negotiation proceeds in three stages. When a price is agreed it is always on deferred payment terms. An initial portion of the cash is paid up front and the seller is required to sign a warranty confirming that the business is exactly as he has stated. After complete take-over, if financial liabilities which were not declared come to light, the seller doesn't get the balance of the sum.

Craig reckons he succeeds in taking over about one in three of the companies he is interested in acquiring. There are a couple of desirable companies he would like to incorporate, but has so far failed to land. "There is one particular company I'd very much like to get hold of, but they don't want to sell to me - at any rate at the price I'm prepared to offer," he says, grinning. "I tend to favour cash generative businesses, with a turn-over of around £1 million. More than that, and the people are usually looking for a great deal of money. Under that figure, prices are more reasonable. One of the important things in acquisitions is to talk informally with some of the staff. Establishing their commitment and attitude is every bit as important as the balance sheet. It's people who make companies."

This year, the acquisitions have continued. The most significant to date has been the purchase of Scotland's Erskine Cleaning Services, which has more than doubled the size of his cleaning division. Its staff numbers about 50, while Erskine will bring to it a workforce of about 80. At the time of going to press, he is also pursuing a take-over which he hopes will result in him becoming probably the youngest chief executive of a company listed on the London Stock Exchange. If that doesn't pan out, he will later this year seek a listing on AIM, the recently launched Alternative Investment Market as a prelude to full London Stock Exchange membership.

Inevitably, in more traditional business circles, his youth causes a few raised eyebrows, although Craig says he doesn't think ageism is a major inhibiting factor in doing business. "Nothing is ever said directly to my face," he says. "There are some organisations which might feel more comfortable dealing with an older person, and if I think that is the case, I'll send in older members of the management team first of all, only becoming involved in the latter stages. I think, dealing with banks, being young probably makes life more difficult. Being in your forties helps. But generally speaking I think my age is a fairly neutral issue. People forget about it when they realise you know what you are talking about, and probably know more than they do on a particular issue."

Pursuing growth through acquisition is an exciting, roller coaster business ride. But no company following that route is ever going to be truly successful unless it develops the capacity and the systems to handle rapid expansion. Another of Craig's skills has been the way he has structured his organisation into separate profit centres, which operate to annual budget and sales targets in a profit-sharing scheme for senior management. He encourages initiative, saying, "If they can work to their budget, they can do pretty much what they want."

Before giving them their head, though, he has been careful to strengthen his executive team. Handling each sector are experienced Directors. He has also recruited a top Finance Director, Ken MacLeod, who has worked with the P &

O Group and PIK International, to oversee the internal systems installed to cope with rapid growth. "Occasionally it's difficult," he admits. "We are growing at such a pace, we have to work very hard to ensure growth doesn't outstrip internal support systems. Structure is very important."

Again because of its fast expansion rate, Craig has been in a position to absorb virtually all the general staff of companies he has taken over, if they wish to stay. Their senior managements, though, are a slightly different proposition; he says it is 50-50 whether they work out. However, he does not embark upon change for change's sake, believing in the old maxim: If it ain't broke, don't fix it. If an acquired company has what he considers to be a good management team in charge of it, only the minimum of re-organisation will be undertaken. "In some cases, all that is needed for companies to perform better is to be part of a larger picture. In others which are under-performing, changes have to be made," he says.

Having occasionally experienced the lash of ageism, he doesn't practise it, himself, at the other end of the spectrum. He considers the big clear-out of middle-aged executives of many firms absolutely crazy, and has no qualms about hiring people 20 to 25 years older than himself. "To build a business of any size, you have to have good people in place and encourage them to make decisions for themselves. You can't build a company on your own. You have to rely on other people, and you need experience as well as youth. I don't agree with ageism. Having said that, we don't have any good management level people under the age of 25. Business should be playing more of a role in training, but to do that they have to get back something tax-wise from the Government. It's very difficult for young people to get started. I'd like to get hold of good young people and train them. I think we should be getting these people as they leave school. Someone going to university to do a business degree would be far better splitting their time between working in a real business environment and study."

That said, it is not an area where Craig has practised what he preaches. Since setting off on the trail of the business big time, he admits to having done only half an accountancy course, preferring to acquire his knowledge in the very practical arena of the negotiating room. Nor is he particularly interested in the high-powered motivational courses staged for businesses, considering them somewhat histrionic. "Part of my job is to motivate staff and I have my own way of doing it," he says quietly. "What motivates people? Money and power - on different scales. People like to live well and to be seen to have a position within an organisation. For example, we don't have a boring company car policy. We give executives a budget and let them buy whatever type of car they want, within that budget. If they want to go out and get a flash model that's fine."

Within the parameters he sets, Craig encourages managerial initiative. Executives are given plenty of latitude to stamp their personalities on their departments, while working towards corporate goals. It is a successful formula, which makes for happy executives. He is also examining ways of broadening out profit-sharing to the wider workforce, although he concedes that expanding it further is a more difficult task. If it ever comes to fruition, it will have to be a system which also educates staff as to their role in the over-all scheme of things.

A believer in de-regulation, he believes that responsible business is more likely to introduce good working practices voluntarily because it is in their own long-term interests to do so, rather than have blanket rules imposed from without, by Government. Hemmed in by too many restrictive regulations, he says, the attitude of business is to defray risk by employing less numbers of staff than they otherwise might take on. He also points out that if business is determined to avoid legislation which it considers to be too heavy-handed, it can usually find ways to circumvent it or negate its effects.

These are not new arguments. In the eternal debate surrounding capitalism and labour, it is hardly surprising the young millionaire comes down so firmly on the side of capitalism. It is the system he has mastered and so skilfully turned to good effect, in the process building up a business which is a substantial Scottish employer. And not without a considerable degree of courage. Even yet, when making an acquisition, in the last seconds before he signs the final cheque, no matter how favourable looking the deal, he always hesitates, asking himself: Am I doing the right thing?

If at board room level business is war by another means - and its terminology of white knights, predators, hostile take-overs and lightning raids all point in that direction - then Craig Whyte may be said to have used his company as a battering ram to breach the gates of the opposition. For him, there remain many more conquests to be made. While there are no certainties in life, it is reasonable to predict that in Vital Holdings plc, we are witnessing the first stages of a young man transforming it into a financial power which will become a world-wide household name.

CHAPTER TWO

Taking a bite of the profit in pets

THERE are some markets which we rarely associate with being big business. One such retail sector is absolutely huge; bigger, possibly, than the whole of the UK's beef industry, and, almost certainly, as large as the country's milk industry. Each year in Britain it commands a spend in the order of £3.4 billion - yet most of us would be hard put to readily identify it.

To translate its magnitude into even more dramatic terms, consider this: Every morning of the working week, at the plant of just one of its principal manufacturers in England, a mile and a half of giant container lorries queue up, nose to tail, to collect its products for delivery across Britain, and for world-wide export.

Have you guessed the industry yet? Let me put you out of your misery: The answer is pet food. Servicing a nation of animal lovers who collectively own some 14 million dogs and cats (7 million of each), it is one of Britain's biggest retail sectors. There is also a sizeable spin-off in pet accessories, from feed bowls and collars to bed baskets, toys and chews.

Nor is our love of pets confined to the four-footed variety. Feed for cage and wild birds also contributes fairly substantially to the market. Indeed, the pet food industry is packed with surprising facts about our generosity towards wildlife. For instance, during winter months, when the ground is frozen, and pickings for wild birds are slim, sales of nuts and bird feed rocket three and four-fold. One Scottish distributor, alone, averages more than 25 TONNES of peanuts a month for wild birds during frosty weather - much of it in the form of bird table feeders or small nets of nuts. As a nation, we probably distribute something in the order of 100 tonnes of nuts per month to our outdoor feathered friends when times are hard.

Against that sort of backdrop, the pet food and accessories market can be seen to be a buoyant, and growing, retail sector.

One of the most successful entrants into it in recent years as a Scottish national wholesaler is Neill Anderson Pet Supplies. Founded in 1989 by husband and wife team Gary Neill, 30, and Carol, 26, it operates from Tor-View, a former mink farm on the outskirts of the picturesque Stirlingshire village of Kippen. In just six years, from a standing start, the couple have taken its annual turn-over from less than £50,000 in the first year to £1.2 million. Selling to pet shops, garages and other outlets across Scotland, Neill Anderson Pet Supplies has secured a Scottish market share of between 12 and 15 per cent of a retail sector which is reckoned, north of the border, to be worth more than £12 million annually. That puts the company among the top four pet supplies wholesalers in Scotland.

The company has a staff of nine and, along the way, as a matter of policy, has contributed substantially to its local rural economy. Gary says: "Every member of staff I have taken on has been unemployed. I won't take someone who is merely looking for a change of job. I want to feel that I have created a new job. I also tend to take people from the rural villages around us, if at all possible."

That commitment to being part of the local community extends even further. The company buys its fuel from the village garage for the transport fleet, even though it knows it could save about £100 a month by installing its own diesel tank; when company reps come calling they are expected to stay overnight at the village hotel. Company postage and stationery needs are met through the local post office. Once, when he and staff had to go to a trade show in Birmingham, travelling to and from England in a single day because of other business commitments, Gary hired the local taxi firm for the round trip. "If there is to be a benefit in spin-offs from our business, I want to see it go into the local community. I feel strongly about this; I believe in doing my bit," he says. "If other companies did the same, we would have a much healthier economic climate in Scotland."

That robust, practical support for the community may be more difficult to sustain when further major expansion and development of the business takes place. But for as long as it is feasible, that company ethos will obtain. Gary's commitment to Kippen and rural Stirlingshire is never in doubt.

At the outset, however, Gary's career path looked set to follow a completely different direction. The youngest of a family of four, he was 10 years of age when his parents moved to Kippen and seemed destined to follow in the footsteps of his father, Archie, who was one of Scotland's most experienced mink farmers. At the time there were some 500 mink farms in Scotland, and Archie was very much the doyen of a booming cottage industry which was well suited to Scotland's climate and agrarian society. He established at Tor-View one of the largest mink farms in Europe which annually reared between 14,000 and 15,000 animals. Gary, who was not scholastically inclined, left Balfron High School at the age of 16, keen to follow in his father's footsteps. Working for the premium end of the market, father and son supplied to the international fur trade high grade pelts which commanded top European prices.

Two factors, above all else, determine the quality of furs which the trade pays for by the square inch - good animal husbandry and diet. Gary explains: "Mink have a fast digestibility rate so to produce good quality furs, nutrition is very important. There are about seven or eight variations on diet in the course of a mink's growth, some of the cycles being as short as three to five weeks. With the wrong diet, you can very easily end up reducing the value of the fur."

As a consequence of that, the mink farm strove to ensure maximum consistency of diet. Unable to buy the balanced nutritional dry feeds they needed for their mink in either the UK or the rest of Europe, the Neills used to import special feeds from the USA. In pursuit of the perfect diet, they tried out special feed rations on selected groups of mink, carefully monitoring food quantities against litter sizes. Given their interest in the subject, they also garnered a very considerable amount of knowledge about the latest research going on into balanced nutrition for animals in general. That was to become an important factor in Gary's eventual change of career, when conditions within the mink fur trade underwent drastic change.

The Danes entered mink breeding in a big way, suddenly flooding the industry with product, much as they were later to do in fish farming. It was, to many peoples' way of thinking, a calculated policy aimed at forcing foreign producers out of business. Before their arrival in the market, in the course of 30 years, world production grew from 24 million pelts to 32 million. In just three years, the Danes forced that figure of 32 million up to 40 million - the equivalent of taking 30 years' profit in just three years. The glut drove down prices sharply, even at the premium end of the market. After three years of disappointing returns, Gary had had enough. It was time, he decided, for a change of tack in his business career.

Joined in a new venture by his girlfriend (later to be his wife), Carol Anderson, who at the time was a 19-year-old design student working with him on the mink farm, the route he chose was to become a wholesaler in pet foods. It may have seemed, on the surface, to be a rather sweeping divergence from his previous trade, but in reality he was capitalising on the knowledge he already had at his fingertips on nutritional needs for animals. While the mink farm was being scaled down, Gary devoted more and more of his time to researching the pet foods business arena.

A handful of other Scottish mink farms, in a bid to generate much needed income, had diversified marginally into pet food wholesaling. But Gary's approach was to be much more radical. With considerable boldness, he had decided that, to break into his chosen new market, the company would begin by launching a brand new "own label" product - a new "all dry" complete dog feed. Manufactured to his own specifications, the meatless feed was wheat-based and came in two versions, one containing higher levels of protein for younger, active dogs, and the other a less protein-packed mixture for older animals. Apart from the dry feeds, which were to be sold under the brand name, Nutra-Mix, the fledgling company was also going to carry a third, more minor line in dry biscuit supplements.

Carol was in full agreement. With the help of a £5000 low interest loan from the Prince's Scottish Youth Business Trust, a charity set up to help young people establish new businesses, the couple set up Neill Anderson Pet Foods Suppliers, taking over part of the farm buildings, owned by Gary's father, as an office and storage area. The company name was a combination of their two surnames. Even at that early juncture, the pattern which still obtains until today, was established: Gary handled the salesmanship, marketing and new product development, while Carol looked after company administration and stock rotation.

To attempt to break into a market dominated by the traditional view that dogs require a meat diet for healthy existence, with a new, and apparently untried meatless product may seem foolhardy. But Gary's reasoning was well founded, if a touch on the ambitious side. From his own research, he knew that complete dry dog food was a vast and growing market. In the USA, 75 per cent of all dogs are fed on dry dog food, and the remainder on canned meat-based dog food. In Britain, the equation is reversed; 75 per cent of dogs are still fed on tinned dog food, while just 25 per cent have been switched to dry nutrition. Given Britain's habit of following US retail trends, the potential for growth in

UK sales of dry dog food was therefore massive.

He also knew, from his mink farming diet experiments, that dry foods - despite the public's general ignorance about them - were a tried and tested form of nutrition which worked extremely well. The selling points in their favour were numerous: Dry foods give dogs an accurate and completely balanced diet every time, with guaranteed levels of vitamin and protein. They are also good for dogs' digestive systems, teeth and gums, eradicating commonplace problems such as bad breath and yellowing teeth. Furthermore, pound for pound weight, they are more economic in price.

All that is in sharp contrast to tinned dog foods, whose manufacturers give only minimum guarantees on protein levels. Moreover, in any canned dog food the principal ingredient is not meat but moisture. It accounts for a quite astounding 76 per cent of content. Nevertheless, the British public has never been fully apprised of the superior benefits of dry dog foods.

No doubt motivated by the higher profit returns on tinned dog food, manufacturers' large advertising spends are concentrated on promoting their canned products, to the virtual exclusion of publicity on dry food alternatives.

However, Gary remains convinced that dry pet foods will come into their own over the next decade. He says: "People have a vision that dogs and cats need meat. Having worked with mink, we always knew that wasn't the case. Dry foods are extremely healthy for animals ... Eventually it is the way the country will go, even though it is happening slowly. It's very much an educational process."

In some ways, though, Gary proved to be a businessman ahead of his time. Five years ago dry pet foods were even less well known than they are now. The young entrepreneur found that trying to wholesale his own brand of a relatively unfamiliar product was a hard sell. It involved considerable expense in producing brochures and leaflets, and - an important consideration for a company covering Scotland with just one salesman on the road (namely Gary) - an equally lengthy investment of time with customers to explain its benefits.

In those early days, the best response came from one of his main target markets, professional kennels. He tried, too, to open up another new market, selling to garage chain forecourts, a move which met with mixed success. Again, he was slightly ahead of market trends. "Many garage chains wrote back saying this wasn't a route they were considering going down," he says. "Now everybody is doing it. They sell everything, including cat and dog food ... I did have a bit of success, though, with some garages, particularly those in more remote areas where they tended to stock everything in the garage shop."

Out on his rounds, Gary very quickly made another discovery: Being a one-product company selling into retail outlets was commercially restrictive. As soon as he had completed his sales pitch on his new brand, back would come the same question from most retailers: What else have you got? It was abundantly clear that, while own brand could get him over the doorway, what was going to keep him there was the ability to offer a much wider range of product. If the company was to properly arrive in the market as a credible wholesaler, it would have to add considerably to its portfolio of goods.

Writing up his customer call cards, Gary noted down what other goods they were interested in buying and immediately began prospecting taking on additional lines from other manufacturers. This was not as easy as it sounds. Contrary to general supposition, a wholesaler does not receive an automatic passport to manufacturers' wares. Indeed, a newcomer to the field very often encounters a certain amount of sales resistance from them. From the manufacturers' perspective, there are several factors to be taken into consideration: Is the new wholesaler credit worthy; is it the sort of organisation they wish to be associated with their product; will the newcomer develop new sales territories or merely service existing ones - possibly undermining long-established distribution deals with other organisations which already sell considerable volumes of their product?

In the selling game, the laws of supply and demand are fluid. For many manufacturers, wholesale distribution is a delicate, if shifting network of competing interests, needs and loyalties. Pricing structures to individual wholesalers vary, dependent upon sales volumes achieved, the types of territories being covered and how badly the manufacturer needs to reach particular markets. By and large, new wholesalers don't encounter an outright No from manufacturers who aren't particularly interested in supplying them - they are merely offered terms on which it is difficult to turn a profit.

All these challenges, Gary very quickly surmounted. Within a matter of months, by dint of contacting manufacturers direct, scouring specialist publications for news of new products, and attending major trade shows, he quickly built up a wide range of product which reduced his reliance on own brand pet food sales. Within 18 months, in fact, the company had completely moved out of its time-consuming own brand product to concentrate entirely on developing other wholesale lines. It had served its purpose.

Gary says: "We used our own product to get a toehold in the market. The product, itself, was good but selling it was still taking up too much time. Also, the profit margin on bulk feed was not as good as the accessory side so we concentrated on building up that area."

Today the company carries an incredible range of 3000 lines in pet foods and accessories. It covers the full gamut of the domestic pet world. From fish tanks, aquatic furniture, electrical water heaters and pumps to hamster cages that glow in the dark; from bird seed, cage ornaments and cages to expanding leads and even expanding beds for dogs and cats; to cages for iguana lizards, all pet lovers' needs are met.

The accessories market is an important adjunct to the business. It has not, however, been developed in any haphazard fashion. Every single line which the company sells is first vetted by Gary. He says: "Everything lands on my desk. Before it is ordered I have to physically see it. The product presentation has to be right and of course it has to be pitched at the right price for the retail outlets."

That attention to detail has always been important to Gary. He says: "Right from the start, the products we chose to list were carefully chosen. We looked at cost, right through to retail prices on them ... I see my job as trying to make retailers' lives as easy as possible. If they are not doing well, we're not doing well. As a company we never forget that. Everything we do is geared to helping retailers sell more easily to customers. On stock availability, we are the best in Scotland. For our retailers we will also go to a lot of trouble in sourcing specific items which their customers have asked for. At times it can be a bit demanding, but I'm convinced it pays dividends."

Over the past few years, there has been one notable change, indicating the company's increased standing as a major Scottish player. Manufacturers are now starting to seek out Gary with new lines, rather than the company having constantly to undertake the hard slog of searching for new product. In the early days, building up a strong suppliers' base was a major exercise. Today the company still regularly updates its stock lists, adding and deleting lines to keep retail interest high, but it is now much better placed to "perk up" sales with regular monthly special offers to its customers.

Gary explains: "Profit comes from margins, but it can also come from turn-over. Although we are not in the volume discount trade, there are times when, by reducing margins, we generate greater turn-over of stock. That increased turn-over can yield better profits than sticking to the original margins. It is very much a question of getting the 'mix' right across the whole range."

At the very heart of wholesaling success lies stock management. Within two years of starting trading, two key developments boosted company growth. The first was the purchase, from Gary's father, of the farm premises, which allowed the couple to embark upon phased increases of storage space. From an original - and most inadequate - 800 sq. ft. the company, through a mix of property adaptations and new building, has grown that figure to 16,000 sq. ft.

The second important development was the introduction of computerised stock records. "There is absolutely no doubt that it progressed us as a company. Investing in information technology has contributed very considerably to growth," says Gary.

Using computerised systems, Carol and Gary are able to monitor stock rotation extremely closely. Gary says: "We employ good business practices here. We constantly monitor stock and how quickly it is turning over. There is actually a financial equation which we employ: Stock holdings divided by turn-over in a particular product, multiplied by margin gives us a figure to which we work. If something isn't turning over quickly enough, either we reduce the stock holding or increase the margin. With computerisation it is possible to break down how much gross and net margin each square foot of warehouse space will generate. That can be further broken down into how much space different products are given, and how much return each will give the company."

The regular, and in-depth, health checks on stock rotation perform a dual function: As well as giving the company the capacity to anticipate and mirror customer demand, the system also provides it with constantly updated information on its true financial performance. That early warning system very quickly flags up any underlying problems - a fairly crucial aspect of wholesaling, where volume of sales can often partially obscure fiscal realities. As Gary says, with a twinkle in his eye, "Turn-over is vanity; profit is sanity."

In growing the company, Gary and Carol were not to desert entirely the field of own product development. In November, 1993, to break into the pet fish market sector, the company bought over Scotland's largest manufacturer of aquariums; they also started to manufacture their own range of aquatic furniture, the smart stands and covers used to set off fish tanks. Backing up Gary's belief that aquarium owners are not given enough variety and choice in what is a £60 million sector, the subsidiary company has concentrated on making aquariums which are highly decorative as well as functional. It now produces fish tanks in a variety of attractive, non-standard shapes for the UK market at retail prices of up to £150. The ornamental stands, too, come in a range of modern colours not generally available. As well as selling fish tanks directly to its own retail customer base, Neill Anderson also supplies them to rival wholesalers across the UK. Perhaps a little surprisingly, it does so on precisely the same terms as it "buys" them from its own subsidiary. "Exactly the same margins are involved," says Gary, "and we ask other wholesalers to stick pretty close to them. In this instance, we are acting as a manufacturing supplier as well as a wholesaler."

With such a wide range of products available, one of the toughest - and most important - tasks is generating product awareness among retailers. Twice a year, the company produces and sends out to traders a large illustrated catalogue detailing every product it handles. This year the company is changing the format. The catalogue is being redesigned to become even more user friendly and will be issued once a year in a special folder. Regular updates of manufacturers' price changes and additional product lines will be sent out as single sheets which can be easily clipped into place.

"Because there's only myself on the road, the catalogue is very much a point of contact with the company. It's our 'face through the door,' " says Gary. "The easier it is to use as a reference book, the better it is for ourselves. When shops have to look up prices or products, we want them to turn automatically to our catalogue, in preference to others. If they use ours, the chances are they will order from us, as well."

It is simple sales psychology, but it works.

Two factors, above all, might be said to characterise the company's steady and solid growth. Firstly, all major company development has been self-financed; secondly, it never enters a new market or offers a major new service to clients unless it is fully confident that the existing staffing and distribution resources are already in place to meet those extra demands. Indeed, on that score, the company actually feels a little more comfortable if it always holds something in reserve, which it can throw in if the situation suddenly warrants it.

However, the company is coming to a number of important cross-roads in its development. Nearly seven years on, Gary is still its only salesman, spending four days out of five on the road servicing accounts. For further growth, the company is going to have to make a decision on how to proceed. "You either go the way of having a sales force who are out selling, which drags in a lot of oncost, or, alternatively, you can reduce your margins slightly and operate what is virtually a tele-sales system, which is what we have done up to now," says Gary. "However, the feeling is that we will have to take on a sales rep to take over new business and a number of the existing accounts."

Equally pressing is a decision on the company's future location. Until now, its growth has been accommodated by what might be described as piecemeal development of its existing site. For the next step forward, that will not be enough. Custom-built warehousing is the only answer. However, the financial logistics of creating from scratch, in open countryside, new premises to house an expanding business are not overly attractive. Apart from the cost involved, the buildings would be a diminishing business asset; if offered for sale, they would never recoup their true value. Gary says bluntly: "As a company we are not prepared to sacrifice more margin for volume from our present site. By spending more capital here, we are not going to get an eventual return on it. The best course for us would be to realise some capital on this site and move."

A more financially feasible option for Neill Anderson is to relocate in the Stirling-Falkirk area, possibly on a secondary business site, in close proximity to the motorway network. Because of the fairly small distances involved, such a move would also permit the business to retain its present staff, an important consideration.

The financial imperatives of commerce are nothing, if not pragmatic. Companies are rarely allowed the luxury of standing still. Almost by definition, if they are not moving forward, they are going backwards. Gary and Carol, having built up a strong distribution service, wholesaling to pet shops, garages and kennels across Scotland, are no exception. They require to continue to expand and diversify to meet the changing complexion of their market place.

Major English manufacturers, having reached saturation levels south of the border, increasingly are looking northwards to develop new volume sales. In Scotland's supermarket chains, the pet food sections are growing larger. Where once they accommodated only dog and cat food, they have expanded into wider realms of pet feeds, accessories and pet care.

Neill Anderson has always stayed out of the high volume market, because it has no wish to find itself becoming almost wholly dependent on servicing a major retail chain's needs. It prefers to keep the "mix" right, with no single customer dominating its distribution service. Today even its largest clients account for no more than four per cent of its total turn-over - a "safety first" precaution against ever becoming over-exposed.

"Superstores will never ever replace the pet shop," says Gary. "Customers going to pet shops rarely just buy something. They are looking for advice and information as well, and retail chains aren't geared to providing that specialist information. But every year the big stores are stealing another little slice of the market."

At his own end of the trade, the market is also fragmenting slightly. More outlets, such as fruit shops, are selling pet products as a secondary line of revenue. For wholesalers like Gary, that eventually may mean more delivery points and smaller loads - a combination which detracts from cost efficiency. Nevertheless, he remains supremely confident that Neill Anderson will continue to grow its Scottish market share. "We can still increase our market percentage," he says. "I think achieving a little more than 30 per cent would be a realistic level."

That represents doubling the size of the present operation, so Gary is constantly on the look-out for new sectors to develop. One he intends to move into soon is horse feed. "That would fit in very comfortably with our present business," he says. "There are numerous stables around the country. The horse-riding set also tend to have dogs as well. There have been one or two people on the agri-side who have moved into dog foods, but no-one has done it from our side of the fence. It would be a trading first in Scotland."

In whatever direction the company moves, it will be very much a joint decision. "We have never been a company to go wild. Everything has been fairly well thought out. I would go so far as to say I'm quite cautious - although Carol would probably laugh at that because she tends to be even more cautious than I am," says Gary. "I tend to be the one thinking up all these ideas, and then we'll go through them together, do some number crunching, and see if they are feasible."

Working together as husband and wife in the same business has not been a problem. "I think being out of the office four days a week probably helps," says Gary frankly. "But there is really a pretty clear division of responsibility.Within the company we've both found roles which we are happy with. Carol would say I probably take more policy decisions than she does - and that's probably true. But then Carol isn't out seeing what is happening. I've got the extra information. On the administration side, I defer to her knowledge. We do work very closely. There's very little on which we don't agree. Even then it's not really a personality clash; it's more sales versus administration. I may want something done a particular way to help customers; Carol might object because it throws an extra workload on her staff. So we always try to strike a balance."

Indeed, striking a balance might be said to be the very ethos of wholesaling: In the juggling of mixed profit margins; in product selection and rotation; and even in the customer base which has been built up. As long as it maintains it, Neill Anderson Pet Supplies, whichever direction it chooses to grow in, is set to go from strength to strength.

CHAPTER THREE

Man with the Midas touch

ONE of the most enduring myths of our times is the phenomenon of the overnight success story. We encounter it regularly in newspapers and magazines chronicling the professional careers of successful men and women. In reality, these articles are little more than modern-day variants of the Cinderella story. Missing from such accounts, or merely paraphrased, are the less dramatic, but character-forming years of slogging it out in obscurity in the foothills, en route to Sugar Mountain. The genuine overnight success story is a rarity. And when it does happen its recipients usually vanish almost as quickly as they arrive on the scene, because theirs is a pre-eminence built upon sand; there is no proper foundation. Within the world of business, the qualities for lasting success remain what they have always been: Good ideas coupled with clear, positive thinking, self-discipline, resilience, perseverance, a capacity for hard work and a lot of common sense. A little luck helps, too. But generally the business breaks happen to those who strive hardest; to a considerable degree in life, we make our own luck. Nevertheless, the myth of the overnight success will continue to be woven through the fabric of our dreams; a nation which so readily invests in the weekly fantasy of winning the National Lottery is not easily deprived of its fairy tales.

One man fated to be linked forever to the "rags to riches" genre is Richard Emanuel, founder and Managing Director of DX Communications, Scotland's largest retailer of mobile phones. And certainly, the success of his company has been nothing short of meteoric.

From being a "one man and his Girl Friday" operation, which began life selling from a former Victorian school turned into a block of commercial units in Govan, Glasgow, DX Communications has streaked ahead of rivals. It is the fastest growing company of its kind in the United Kingdom, opening branches across Scotland at the rate of virtually one a month. One in four of all new mobile phones in Scotland is bought from a DX outlet or from its central support office. It currently has 18 High Street retail outlets, and employs a large - and continually growing - staff of of more than 200. It is also developing internationally. In a lightning foray into Europe, virtually overnight it has become the largest mobile phone retailer in Holland, and is about to expand into both Belgium and France. In five short years the annual turn-over of the company has rocketed from £90,000 to an estimated £25 million in 1996. Its mainland Europe expansion will probably add another £10 million to that total. Even within a business sector which, itself, is one of the fastest growing anywhere on earth, that is a phenomenal achievement, made all the more impressive by the youth of the man at the helm of the company. Richard Emanuel is just 28.

Yet his success cannot be explained away merely by the fact that, looking around for a growth business sector in which to seek a career, he got in on the ground floor of the communications industry in anticipation of the boom which was about to happen. It has as much to do with the business philosophies he embraced during his formative years, and the team of senior executives whom he has gathered around him to take the company forward. The development of DX Communications is fascinating because what sets it apart from its competitors is one man's ability to imbue heavyweight executives in the industry with an enthusiasm and belief in his personal vision, while his company was no more than a "minnow" in a pool rapidly filling with big fish, and not a few sharks.

After listening to him expound his ideas, one threw in his lot with Richard to become a partner in an amalgamation of their two businesses under the DX Communications name (even though Richard's company was only marginally the larger of the two). The second key executive was "head hunted" from a well-established corporate marketing career with the Securicor group, one of the communication industry's market leaders. On the promise of a tranche of shares in the tiny company, at a time when it had opened only a single retail outlet, he took a drop in salary to join DX Communications.

To gain for his fledgling enterprise two heavyweight players, more normally to be found talking corporate marketing and technical investment decisions in the Boardrooms of the industry's leading companies, demonstrated, on Richard Emanuel's part, salesmanship of the highest order. It also exhibited exceptionally high confidence in where the small company was going. But then the young entrepreneur has never been short on self-belief. He says: "I have always believed I would achieve something. Even when I didn't have a clear idea of what I wanted to do, something inside of me always told me that I would."

Whatever that "something" was to be, it did not make itself readily apparent during his school days. Brought up on the south side of Glasgow, Richard was enveloped in a strongly educational family background. His English-born father was a chemistry lecturer at the University of Glasgow; his Canadian mother a Further Education teacher at the city's Langside College. Richard, himself, attended the fee-paying Hutchesons' Grammar School in Glasgow. As academics, his parents were both keen that he go on to university to gain a degree, but Richard had other ideas. School failed to hold his interest. For him the classes lacked focus because they were not geared to any specific goal with which he could relate. Unsettled and restless, despite his parents' considerable misgivings, he left, aged 17. Rather than do a sixth year at the grammar school, he enrolled at Langside College, which was slightly more commercially oriented, to study the leisure industry.

It was the mid-eighties, the height of a Scottish fitness boom, and as befits a well set up, 6ft. 4ins teenager, who used to command the number 8 jersey for his school rugby team, Richard was interested in sports and fitness. On leaving college, he gained a job as a trainee manager for the Dave Greenhills chain of health clubs. It proved a red-blooded introduction to the world of business. At the time nearly all the literature concerning the health and fitness industry came from the USA, where it was truly big business, well organised, well developed and bristling with all manner of statistical, psychological and motivational selling tools. For the first time Richard was exposed to the almost evangelistic fervour of doing business the American way. Being preached were the virtues of pro-active business methods; specific organisational techniques; staff and client motivation; marketing; salesmanship and a host of positive-minded lifestyle and commercial attitudes.

His boss being a forward-thinking businessman who believed in pushing staff hard, but positively, stretching their self development, Richard regularly would find on his desk stacks of reading material to absorb, giving him a thorough knowledge of the health and fitness industry covering its many aspects, from physique to nutrition. There was also a wide range of business books which were required reading. Some might have found such in-depth immersion overpowering. To the teenager it was utterly fascinating. For him, a completely new window had been opened up on the world of business. It was a perspective which was exciting; it was positive; it invited personal growth; it embraced challenge and adventure; it was highly focused, an exercise of business as a totality vision. Moreover, it was results-driven. To an impressionable and enthusiastic teenager, it must have seemed as if Charles Atlas had switched from producing body-building techniques to writing thrilling, "how to do it" business manuals. The "sock it to 'em," clear-cut attitudes expressed in the literature were, in fact, the seed corn of his own business philosophies, which were to mould his activities in later years. Today, asked to name his business heroes, he lists among them Mark McCormack, John Harvey Jones, Scottish philanthropist Andrew Carnegie, Richard Branson and, most of all, Kwik-Fit's Tom Farmer. "There were a lot of other business influences in the early days when I was getting started," he says. "Many people gave me support and good advice; I absorbed information from many sources. I believe we were given two ears and just one mouth for a very good reason."

Back then, however, as an 18-year-old, he was happy to soak up the information, absorbing the attractive, go-getting methodology culled from American business, while having an enjoyable, if not overly well paid, lifestyle. For a teenager, a fitness club was a very pleasant, sociable working environment. With a common bond of interest in sports and fitness, the public using the clubs were an interesting cross-section of society, ranging from company managing directors to folk on the dole. "They were a good bunch of people," he recalls. "The good thing about the job was you were forced to interact with a wide variety of people from very different backgrounds. It wasn't a mixed club - men and women had their own separate training days - so there weren't any poseurs hanging around. I worked in three separate branches of the company to gain experience."

It was excellent training. With some 10 to 12 staff under his authority, he had to acquire all the management skills required in running a small business, save for the bookkeeping. With a throughput of 300 to 500 people per week, he had to keep on top of club maintenance and presentation, as well as selling and marketing it to potential new members. For him, it was a happy, two-year interlude, before moving on to the larger Olympic health club chain founded in Glasgow by Hugh Sweeney. Hailing from the Midlands, Sweeney was another boss who believed in management through staff development.

Richard was appointed manager of the group's largest and most profitable club in Pollokshaws Road. With a staff of 20, a membership running into the thousands, and about 100 new members being enrolled every week, Richard's salesmanship and management talents expanded. It was a job where the technique was to sell the sizzle rather than the sausage. "You weren't actually selling a product, you were selling the benefits of health and fitness," he says. "Most of the new membership came through referrals so we had our minds geared to generating referrals from satisfied customers."

After a year, however, though still enjoying the job and the responsibilities of running a busy club, Richard decided it was time to switch careers, seeking out something completely different in mainstream business. At one time he might very well have stuck with the health and fitness leisure industry, in hopes of eventually opening his own chain of clubs, but there were sound, practical reasons behind his change of heart.

The health and fitness boom, at the level he could hope to enter it, was beginning to taper off. Only months after leaving his first club, the Greenhills group had gone out of business, which must have planted some doubts in his mind: If a chain run so professionally by his former business mentor couldn't make it, then what future was there for that type of operation? The second reason was financial. Now of an age when he was beginning to look to the future, he wanted to become involved in something which was well paid and offered good financial prospects.

He had no clear idea of what that was going to be. With a precocity beyond his 21 years, he sat down and analysed the situation, asking himself the following questions: What business sectors out there are fast moving? Where are there going to be a lot of opportunities and potential? The answer he came up with, from studying the business sections of newspapers, was the comm - unications industry.

Today he says of that fateful decision, which was to place him on the road to creating one of Scotland's fastest growing retail businesses: "Yes, it was as analytical as that. I had zero information on the subject. But it didn't take a huge amount of intelligence to see that the communications industry was going to expand. The growth in the use of phones and faxes, and the deregulation of British Telecom all pointed in that direction."

In that statement, he does himself less than justice. For all that within the industry giant conglomerates were pouring billions of pounds into both its infra-structure and product development, in a frantic race against one another, the general public was largely oblivious to the explosion of new communications technology. Cable and satellite TV - the most public face of the developments - had been painfully slow to attract a strong viewing base and were regarded as mega-million pound flops. In phone communications, even with the arrival of deregulation, no-one seriously expected anyone to challenge the supremacy of British Telecom. It was widely regarded as an unassailable business monopoly which had merely transferred from the public to the private sector. Mobile phones were looked upon as little more than expensive yuppie toys. It was to be at least three years before the public began to become truly aware of the extent of the information technology revolution going on under its nose. Richard Emanuel, with no more information than anyone else to call upon, had made the first in a series of exceptionally far-reaching business decisions which were to have an enormous impact upon his life and eventually his company.

Having chosen his business sector, the next stage was to learn everything he could about it. Through a friend of a friend, he gained an introduction to Cellex Communications, a Paisley company, now defunct, which sold a wide variety of products, including cellular phones and fax machines. It took him on as a salesman. Some of the business leads were generated by the company's tele-sales staff, but in the main, Richard's job was to go out "cold calling" on firms. His beat was principally small to medium-sized companies. And it was a very different world from the one to which he had been accustomed. As Richard freely admits, "It's lonely going out on the road selling, especially having moved to it from an environment where every day you worked with friends."

However, to make the transition easier for himself, he put into practice the positive mind techniques he had so often read about. Trudging round an average of 50 companies a day, seeking sales, he adopted its self-motivational methods. Instead of focussing upon rejections - which comprised a dispiriting 95 per cent of his calls - he looked at the exercise in a completely different way. Having calculated what commission he was earning from his 5 per cent success rate, he worked out that every call - whether successful or not - was actually earning him £4. Viewed from that perspective, it became much easier to retain enthusiasm and self-confidence when making his rounds, and Richard began genuinely to enjoy the challenge. "It is hard on shoe leather, but it works," he says. "A lot of business is number crunching. You are playing percentage success rates, so you have to try and rationalise what you are doing. You condition your mind. It's good training because you do get a lot of rejections."

For more than a year, Richard worked in Paisley, learning the business and saving hard to achieve another ambition, an extended visit to Canada. At the back of his mind was the idea that he might emigrate. It was a country which, in many ways, was a second home to him. Like many Canadian "exiles," his mother made a point of regularly travelling back to see her family, and many of Richard's school holidays had been spent in the Vancouver area, visiting relatives. Richard loved the trips, and meeting his mother's large North American family. In particular, he hero-worshipped his uncle, Glen Metcalfe. A colourful, larger than life character who epitomised the North American pioneering spirit, he had begun his working life at 15 down the silver mines of British Columbia; moved to Manitoba to build up from nothing a successful 4,500-acre farm before selling up and moving back to Vancouver, where he built up an equally successful construction business. He was a man of great energy, drive and self-belief, who bulldozed through obstacles, believing anyone could achieve whatever they wished, if they wanted it badly enough - and were prepared to get off their butt and work for it. Richard's intention was to work for his uncle, taking whatever type of job was available, and prospect business opportunities.

For three months, he did just that. He and his uncle got on famously, and became very close. Everything was going to plan, save for one thing Richard hadn't bargained on: He was deeply and permanently homesick. "I couldn't believe how incredibly homesick I was," he says. "There I was in one of the most beautiful cities in the world, a really exciting, booming place with loads of opportunities, and I was missing Scotland and the people."

The feeling didn't lessen, so Richard returned to Scotland. What the Canadian experience had done, however, was to fire him with a renewed ambition to make something of his life. "There is no doubt that Canada was the catalyst for me," he says. "It was a combination of things - the 'can do' attitude of the people, and my uncle's approach to life. Having worked with him, and having seen the way he operated, I was determined I was going to do something worthwhile."

Back in Scotland, he was re-engaged as a salesman by his old firm, from which he had departed on excellent terms. This time, however, his sights were set firmly on starting his own business. Every free moment was spent planning his future. In November, 1990, he quit the firm to form DX Communications. The origins of the company name lay very much in the motivational business literature he so much admired - the D stood for determination, the X for expectation to achieve. On 14th January, 1991, DX Communications opened for its first day of business.

The intervening two months had been busy ones. Having spent more cash than he had intended in Canada, Richard's funds were limited. He had £1,300 in savings. To augment that capital, he went to his own local Bank of Scotland branch, where he was an ordinary customer, and through its assistant manager, arranged a £3,000 business overdraft facility. For premises, he took a small unit within Govan Work Space. The location chose itself. Devoted primarily to small, start-up companies, it leased space cheaply on a month to month basis. There he was joined in the new venture by Rae MacDonald, one of the girls from his old firm, who had told him she wanted to come to work for him. Rae, who is still with the company today, handled the office administration and manned the company's solitary phone while Richard went out knocking company doors and drumming up customers.

In the beginning it was a hand to mouth existence. As a new trader, it was difficult for Richard to obtain credit facilities from manufacturers. Most insisted on DX Communications paying Cash On Delivery for equipment. Richard would first have to pre-sell to business clients, then when the order was clinched, order the item from the manufacturer, pay for it, and deliver it a few days later to the customer. It was a cumbersome method, costly in both time and resources, but the young entrepreneur had little choice in the matter. However, there was a plus side. The prices of cellular phones, at that time, had yet to tumble to their present levels. They cost in the region of £300 to £400, so there was a reasonable mark-up on every sale.

Even so, money was extremely tight. There were to be more than a few months when Richard had to forego any salary because the business couldn't afford to pay him. From the start, DX Communications dealt in an exceptionally wide range of products, on the basis that anything the company sold was turn-over, and hopefully profit. It may have seemed a rather scatter-gun approach, but there was another important reason for travelling that route: Sales of any description, big or small, introduced the company to new clients at a time when widening its customer base was a crucial stage of its development. Although he was in the phones business, Richard remembers being so keen to generate cash flow that he sold a 28-inch screen television, which was in the same catalogue, to a pub in Duke Street, Glasgow. "I went staggering into the pub with this huge set, and the guy wanted me to install it. I hadn't a clue about the controls," he says.

In its first year of trading, DX Communications achieved a turn-over of £90,000. By the time the second year came along, DX Communications was trying to focus its selling operations more and more on the cellular phone market. Reading the industry's trends, Richard realised that, as mobile phones dropped in price, they were becoming less of a business tool and more of a people product. The general public was buying them in greater numbers for a host of different reasons. For some, a mobile phone was a safety precaution to have in their cars in case of breakdowns; for others they were a convenience, particularly in remote areas where public telephones were few and far between. Having got into the habit of using them, they became an indispensable part of their lifestyles. With reception coverage of the country constantly being improved and expanded, he foresaw mobile phones becoming a major area for commercial growth.

Having reached those conclusions, from them flowed certain business imperatives. Chief among them was establishing a proper retail outlet. But the company, which by now had a staff complement of six (four in sales, two in administration), was still too small to make that jump. It didn't have any after-sales service back-up of its own, and was reliant upon manufacturers for repairs and technical support. In another of those periodic, but very large decisions, Richard decided to attempt to acquire that extra capacity in one fell swoop by proposing a merger between his own company and that of John Whyte, who ran his own communications company from a nearby commercial unit. Their combined strengths, he believed, stood to achieve a great deal more than operating independently.

The two men already knew each other. Twenty years Richard's senior, John was an electrical engineer to trade, who had set up his own company to advise on and install communications systems for firms. Like Richard, he was still trying to grow his business. When the two had first encountered each other in the car park outside their respective units, as semi-rivals in the same market, they had eyed each other up rather warily, but that reserve had quickly dissipated as, from time to time, they borrowed pieces of equipment from each other. They discovered they got on together extremely well. Once the initial overture had been made, the two sat down and thrashed out a deal which was finalised in September, 1992. Under it, John's own company staff - there were four - and business operations became part of DX Communications, in return for him becoming a director and gaining a shareholding in the company. It was an inspired move. "John brought a lot of strengths to the business," says Richard. "He was very good at organisation and the infra-structures of companies. Because of his background he was also much better than me on technical matters. He had strength in depth on the technical side, while I was strong on the sales side. We were a very good fit."

Over the next few months, they worked towards their first joint company goal, transferring DX Communications to Pollokshaws Road, where it would have, for the first time, a retail shop. In January of the following year the move was made. Within months of the shop being opened, Richard made another quantum leap - by setting out to "head hunt" Chris Gorman, then a corporate business manager within the Securicor group. With a 40 per cent stake in Cellnet, Securicor, through its subsidiary, Securicor Cellular Services, was - and is - one of the communications industry's big players. It supplied equipment to DX Communications. Richard had met Chris on a number of occasions and had been greatly impressed by his abilities. He and John set about bringing him into the company as marketing and sales director. Following a series of protracted meetings, the young marketing executive finally agreed to join the company on a lower salary, but with a shareholding in the business. "Bringing Chris on board was a key factor in DX's growth and development," says Richard. "Chris is a sales and marketing whizzkid; a real dynamo. In fact, it was the addition of both John and Chris that was the real catalyst in DX's growth."

At the time, though, it was an exceptionally bold stroke. For the size of company it then was, Chris's arrival meant DX Communications was extremely top heavy in executive talent. Although the three men all had different executive functions to perform, the business infra-structure was too small to properly separate them. Even physically there wasn't room for them. At the new HQ in Pollokshaws Road, nearly every inch of space had been devoted to the shop and its storage area. The premises were so small that the three executives were forced to time-share a single, tiny office - a claustrophobic cubby-hole created out of a walk-in cupboard, from which the door had been removed to allow in a little air and light. Packing his large frame into that dismal space was nightmarish for Richard. "You didn't want to be in that cupboard too long," he recalls. "Every so often I had to go out into the street for a breath of air and some daylight because I couldn't stand it any more."

In large organisations there is frequently a clash of egos between senior executives as they jostle for power and influence for their own divisions or departments. It speaks volumes for the personal bond which existed within the DX management team that, in such cramped quarters, living in each other's pockets, they got on so well together professionally. They were an exceptionally close-knit team, which goes a long way to explaining the success of DX Communications.

"I had a vision of where the company was going, and I knew that business was all about people," says Richard. "If you can get the best people into your business, then you succeed. These were expensive guys. But if they could take a drop in salary and have a bigger role in a smaller company, then they were sharing in that vision. Why did they come? I suppose because of my enthusiasm and the senior posts they were offered in the business. You can't fake enthusiasm - people see through it. I had a passionate belief in where the company was going. By the same token, they made a judgement about me. Both of them had more to risk than I did. If things didn't work out I could always dust myself down and start over. They both had family responsibilities. For them it was a big commitment. But they knew the industry's potential. Since coming into the company, they have made as big a contribution as I have. They took the vision and drove it further. They put their heart and soul into the business - and we still get on very well."

The year 1993 might well be described as a watershed in the company's growth. All the building blocks were in place for expansion. They coincided, too, with another watershed, this time in the communications industry, itself. By the end of 1993 UK mobile phone tariffs were radically altered. In addition to the normal £25 monthly business tariff, a £15 per month price band, aimed at less frequent users, was introduced, setting the stage for explosive growth within the general public. Almost alone among small, but developing companies, DX Communications had a heavyweight, experienced management team in place ready to meet that challenge head-on. The company was expanding, virtually in all directions.

Its turn-over having risen by 100 per cent in its second year to £180,000, in its third year the company began opening new retail outlets across the country, ploughing back into the business every penny of profit it made. During 1993 and 1994 DX mobile phone centres started arriving on the High Streets of Scotland with such regularity that it was as if they were being run off an assembly line - which indeed in a way they were. The company very quickly knew the exact amount of floor space needed for optimum profitability, and where the sites should be located. It was a slick, practised operation geared to drive company turn-over first to £800,000 in its third year, then £4 million in 1994. The year 1995 saw that figure treble to £12 million; and DX is now well on course to more than double that figure in 1996.

On another front, the company was also busy creating the infra-structure to back up its retail operations. Believing firmly that at the core of the business there should be in-depth after-sales care and technical support available to customers, Richard set out to provide it. In 1994, DX bought over at a reasonable price a small technical company,Westwood Communications, Clydebank, which was about to cease trading. Today its 14-strong staff form the hub of a dedicated technical support division for company operations. That additional capacity has in turn given rise to new spin-offs, such as a general repair service to other communications companies throughout the UK, plus repairs of phones under manufacturers' warranty. It has also slashed the turn-around on customer repairs from three or four weeks to a maximum of 48 hours - a figure DX is continuing to improve upon. It also bolstered another vitally important strand of the business, the sale of accessories, parts and batteries. In the communications retail world, profits accrue from just about everything else other than the actual sales of mobile phones. With a strong service base, DX was assured of customer loyalty and repeat business.

The third major plank in expansion was yet another move, at the end of 1993, this time to establish a central support office combining all the key functions in 5,000 sq. ft. of office space within a commercial complex in Durham Street, Kinning Park. The £250,000 refurbishment of such spacious premises, taken on a 15-year lease, was, to say the least, unnerving. Richard recalls: "It was really embarrassing. We held a special company night to mark the move. At the time we hadn't all that many phone centres up and running - I think we had about four - and there weren't nearly so many central support office staff. The place was huge, and even though we tried to place staff carefully, they looked like peas rattling round in a bucket. You could tell what people were thinking when they came in the door: What has this lunatic gone and done? Now, of course, it's comical thinking back to that time because we're packed like sardines, even after taking on another 2,000 sq. ft. of space. However an awful lot of people, clients included, thought I'd over-reached myself."

The arrival in Durham Street was to herald more significant developments within the company, beyond High Street retail expansion. The company was able to diversify its operations, maximising profitability, by rapidly creating a substantial tele-sales division, which led naturally to development of a mail order service. DX Communications has also a well established corporate business division, which is a large and important aspect of company activities. From the Durham Street centre it was also able to develop a hire division renting out short and long-term hire equipment to companies who needed it for an extensive range of special projects.

In 1994, as the phenomenal rate of expansion continued, more business coups were achieved. The one Richard takes most pride in is the company being awarded Britain's very first mobile phones "Oscar." In March of that year, in competition against more than 2000 British companies, DX Communications was voted Best UK Dealer of the Year by Cellnet, in the country's first mobile phone industry awards. The company was also named Best Scottish Retailer. The twin success in such a prestigious event, for Richard, was heady wine, indeed. It was recognition by his peers that in an extremely competitive industry that DX Communications was a force to be reckoned with; it had truly arrived. The awards also generated valuable publicity across Britain. The night they learned of their triumph, though, there was no big champagne celebration. "Back at the hotel, we just sat around drinking tea. We were shattered; emotionally drained at achieving such an honour. I think we were all in bed by 9.30," says Richard.

In the fairly complex world of the mobile phone industry, some general background is required to appreciate the full significance of just how far DX Communications has come. The mobile phone industry is a market which exists in separate layers. At its core are the networks which provide the infrastructure to transmit calls through a series of private transmitters dotted across Britain. There are four rival networks, the two biggest being Cellnet, which is jointly owned by British Telecom and the Securicor group, and Vodafone, which is wholly owned by the Vodafone Group plc. Their networks each cover about 98 per cent of the country. In third place comes the Orange network. A newcomer on the scene, it was set up by Hutchison Telecom in 1994, and reaches more than 80 per cent of the country. The final player is Mercury One-2-One, a small network which operates in the south of England.

The networks sell their airtime to the next layer in the business chain, a series of special companies known as service providers. They are in charge of connecting mobile phone users to the network of their choice. It is they who send out the monthly bills to customers and devise the tariffs, usually within guidelines suggested by the various networks, although, because they have bought the airtime, they can and do impose their own airtime rates. In recent years the number of service providers has contracted rapidly as the larger players swallow up the smaller companies. Over a four-year period, from a high of more than 100 service providers, numbers have fallen by two-thirds. By the end of 1996 it is expected there will be only about 10 to 20 large billing companies servicing phone users.

The final layer of the industry is provided by High Street retail companies like DX Communications. DX supplies the full range of phones used on all rival networks to customers and offers them impartial product information across the board. Its principal profits, however, are derived not from phone sales, but from the special introduction fees they receive from the Big Three - Cellnet, Vodafone and Orange - for every phone user they bring to their networks. This subsidises the price the customer pays for his or her mobile phone. The final choice of phone and network, of course, always lies with the customer, but on phones they get an excellent deal, paying only a fraction of their true retail value.

These days, DX has boosted its annual advertising spend to around £1.5

million, an extremely important development for the company because of the rapidly changing complexion of the market. Every year that passes, the switch from business to private consumers becomes more pronounced. By the year 2000, if current trends continue, there will be 800,000 Scots using mobile phones, compared to a mere 55,000 in 1993. The current sales split for DX is already 25 per cent business, 75 per cent domestic users. In an increasingly general consumer-led market, big budget advertising will largely determine where those customers will buy their phones. By investing so heavily in advertising, DX Communications, once again has got itself into the arena ahead of the pack.

In the past two years, while consolidating its internal operational systems, the company has still managed to surprise its rivals. It was widely expected, in the next stage of its growth, to begin battling its way into the more mature, and fairly crowded English market. Instead, DX Communications jumped the Channel, and targeted Holland. It was a lightning strike. In just seven weeks, DX formed a new company, Dexcom, leased and moved into premises at Hoofdorp, near Amsterdam, and recruited an all-Dutch staff to man its continental central supply office, save for two experienced British executives put in to run operations.

The move arose out of a joint venture suggested by Tom Farmer, the founder of Kwik-Fit, the international tyre and exhaust fitting group which has a substantial chain of 130 depots in the country. Within hours of flying over to Holland to prospect the market, Richard realised he was in a country ripe for development. Only 3 per cent of the Dutch population use mobile phones, which is one of the lowest rates in Europe, and well behind UK levels of 10 per cent. The country was also in the throes of a deregulation exercise remarkably similar to that which Britain had undergone and the language barrier was minimal; in Holland nearly everyone speaks excellent English as well as Dutch.

DX Communications went ahead with a major joint promotion with Kwik-Fit, supplying mobile phones to its Dutch depot customers, then went on to fix up a deal to obtain retail space in 130 fast photo shops owned by Super Photo, Holland's largest one-hour development company. Overnight, DX sprang into the Dutch market as the country's biggest mobile phone retailer. It also intends to provide Holland with its own technical service back-up. "It was too good an opportunity to miss," says Richard. "That's why we moved with such speed. Besides, Holland is only 20 minutes further away than London by plane."

Having made such an impact on Holland, it is now setting its sights firmly on Belgium and France, where again mobile phone ownership is much lower than in the UK. Further down the line, the company may consider franchising in England. Although still relatively small in Britain, franchising now accounts for something like 65 per cent of new business start-ups in the USA. It is perceived to be the answer to statistics there which show that only one in five new businesses survive the first five years, and of those survivors, only one in five are still in business at the end of the next five-year term. Where America leads, Britain tends to follow. The trend towards franchising within the UK, particularly from indigenous companies, is likely to be a growing one.

Another good reason for DX Communications eventually to consider the franchising route in England, apart from the smaller risk factor involved, is that it forces the franchise company to ensure its servicing infra-structure is in good order. One of the greatest challenges faced by DX in its exceptionally fast development has been the danger of it outstripping itself and swamping its infra-structure with too many demands. While instituting its own in-house staff training programmes, and achieving ISO9002 standards and manufacturer approval for its technical services, it has been a fairly constant tightrope walking exercise. The company has always grown organically. If it decides to enter the franchise market it will be forced to take a long, hard look at further consolidation of its operations, imposing new disciplines and improving existing internal delivery systems, right across the board.

If the yardstick of success is a company's ability to respond to change, then DX Communications has shown itself to have that quality in abundance. In a market which seems to be expanding exponentially, it is not always easy to divine the best way forward; the array of new technology being developed inevitably will throw up more than a few commercial dead ends. DX Communications' skill, to date, has been to make several extremely crucial decisions in advance of some of those developments, which have placed it in the right part of the market at the right time.

In some ways, the wheel has turned full circle. On retail, DX is back to selling a range of office technological equipment, as well as mobile phones. This time, though, it has bulk buying muscle at its disposal. It is difficult to predict where the communications industry will be in a decade, save to say it will be bigger and even more diverse. The analogue phone is gradually giving way to the digital one. We can now hook a mobile phone to a fax machine or a computer and send information to any phone in the world. Who knows what new voice or micro-technology will bring? In a decade or so, we may all be wearing personal phones like wristwatches. If that ever happens, the chances are a sizeable proportion of them will have been sold to us by DX Communications or its European operation, Dexcom.

CHAPTER FOUR

Sue's a pioneer in multi-media

IT IS one of the paradoxes of life that the greatest revolution in communication there has ever been in the history of the human race makes us less, rather than more, confident in our daily working lives. We feel less in control.

Confrontation with new technology induces in many of us a feeling of inadequacy, if not outright alienation. Very few of us are even halfway computer literate. We learn precisely the business systems we require to know to get us through our working day, and not a jot more. If something beyond our smattering of experience crops up, we send for a specialist. We are therefore uncomfortable around change. Just when we come to terms with one set of new working practices, something else often radically different - and important - hoves in view on the horizon. As old dogs, we resent constantly having to learn new tricks.

The extreme rapidity of change in computer technology and its applications has undoubtedly ratcheted the pace of all our lives up several gears. In business, in commerce, finance and politics, we are required to respond more quickly to situations than ever before. There is no hiding place. The mobile phone with the business query at the other end rings as easily at the top of Ben Nevis as it does in the heart of a city office. The over-spent Scottish credit card proffered in payment for a bill is as routinely exposed in a few nano-seconds in New York as it is in Edinburgh, and has been for quite some time.

Indeed, because of the fast reactions of our information systems, it is more than probable that computers contributed mightily to London's "Black Wednesday" Stock Market crash of the eighties, when something like 25 per cent of the trading value of shares was wiped out in a single day. With financial systems pre-set to automatically sell stock falling to certain price lows, the human element so important to commerce was largely missing in the landslide of shares divestment.

In the relationship between mankind and its most powerful machine, the computer, it remains a moot point who is master and who is servant ... there will now be a short pause while those who wish to stop the world and get off, proceed to do so in an orderly fashion.

Fortunately for us latter-day Luddites, who given half the chance would cheerfully uninvent scientific development and in a trice roll back the boundaries of technological progress to more personally manageable proportions, such drastic action as a planetary exit isn't necessary. The software and hardware designers, themselves, recognise the necessity of overcoming the learning barriers, both real and psychological, which exist between ourselves and our technology.

It is no accident that the term, "user friendly," has passed into common usage. Making software easier and simpler for us to operate is a constant objective. Where once a series of commands had to be memorised, a single key stroke or touch of the screen suffices. It has led to the jibe that we are creating a "monkey see, monkey do" culture, where people carry out work functions with no clear understanding of what they are doing, or of the principles involved behind those functions.

There is more than a grain of truth in that assertion. What it all boils down to, though, is the need to find better ways to teach people. The reality is that never, at any point in history, has a general public been required, right across the board, to undertake such steep learning curves to stay abreast of normal living. In industry, commerce and just about every aspect of business life, the demand for specialist or multi-skilled personnel has never been higher. Equally, the need for improved education and information delivery systems to help people more effectively acquire those skills has never been greater.

The most successful educational and information systems are those which set out to free people from the tyranny of too rapid technological change and an overload of information - ones which permit them to learn at their own pace, in a way in which they feel completely comfortable. These systems are known as inter-active multi-media systems.

The Next Generation

Most of us have encountered the term, but - true to form in our half-knowledge of computer technology - would be hard put to define it. Here is one definition: A multi-media system is an infinitely flexible method of supplying one-to-one computerised learning and information programmes on any subject.

For a moment, think of a training manual or a volume of an encyclopaedia - then imagine that the information contained on every page has been translated into computerised visual terms, using the techniques of the TV and cinema industry. Film, speech, sound, music, animated graphics, diagrams, zoom photography, coloured photograph stills and the printed word are all employed in a single learning programme. That is the "multi-media" part.

Now imagine you are sitting in front of a computer screen, calling up this "visual book." Obviously you don't want to view all its contents, because that would take hours, if not days. So you flip to any subject you wish to see within it, simply by placing your finger on the touch-sensitive screen of your TV console, in response to a menu of choices. That is the "inter-active" part.

In essence, inter-active multi-media systems are multi-layered training or information films where the viewer chooses what he or she wishes to see. Their applications are quite literally limitless. They can be used equally well as a specialist teaching or training tool, or as a method of getting information across to the public on anything from health education to housing availability. In public places, such as shopping malls and airports, more simplified versions can be used to tell you where a particular shop lies or, if you are a tourist from abroad, what number of bus you must catch to reach a specific hotel, what accommodation price range it is in - and tell you in your own language.

One of the great benefits of multi-media systems is their flexibility. Information can be easily and cheaply updated, added to or replaced.

But what is really important about multi-media systems is that they supply information in a way which breaks down many of our personal inhibitions towards using new technology. In the field of education, where they were first largely dismissed as a glitzy high-tech teaching fad, and now in training, evaluations show they are an extremely effective way of dispensing information. Because multi-media systems engage us (and most of our senses) as active participants, our retention levels are often higher than those achieved by conventional methods. If one picture is worth a thousand words, it is a quantum leap to the value of one moving picture, plus animated graphics, sound, music and a score of other attention-grabbing cinematic devices.

It is not over-stating matters to predict that multi-media systems are going to revolutionise, at the very least, the world's training methods. By the early part of the next century, multi-media programmes are going to be one of the most universally used training tools around. Internationally, they are already big business. In the USA, in sharp contrast to our own almost negligible figures, nearly 70 per cent of all workers have already used a multi-media system for training in their job. That demand will continue to grow.

Although still in their infancy in Britain, in terms of companies and organisations using them, it is safe to predict that in this country, too, multi-media systems are about to explode on the business scene. One statistic pointing firmly in that direction is the calculation that by the year 2000, half of the United Kingdom's multi-million pound training budget will be spent on information technology. A huge proportion of that cash will be devoted to the development of computerised training programmes. In the face of its already expanding international use, Britain - and Scotland - simply can't afford to be left behind.

Fortunately for Scotland, which like the rest of the UK has come relatively late to the development and marketing of this potentially boom technology sector (as a nation, we are about five years behind North America), we do have an important toe-hold in its applications.

Almost from the start, an Edinburgh-based company, Broad Knowledge Systems, has been most impressively trail-blazing world-beating innovations in the field. From offices within the labyrinthine basement of Radio Forth's headquarters in the Capital, in a rather neat reversal of history, Broad Knowledge Systems has been a case of its Canadian-born founder, Sue Cook, coming from the New World to the Old, as a pioneer.

Although just 27, Sue and her husband Mark, 29, who later joined her in Broad Knowledge Systems, have kept the company very much up at the cutting edge of information technology, while steadily growing the business. How they have done so is an interesting commercial case history; indeed it is nothing short of a triumph. Most businesses sell products and services which, by and large, are alternatives to something else that is on the market; the prospective buyer has some general familiarity with what is on offer. That has not been the case for Broad Knowledge Systems.

From its incorporation as a business, within Scotland it has been charting unknown commercial territory. Before it could even start its job of educating people through its multi-media information systems, it first had to educate potential purchasers about what they were. In selling, there is no harder task for a fledgling company to undertake than marketing a completely unknown type of product to a country which isn't even aware of the commercial sector in which it exists, far less what products or services it contains.

The Next Generation

It is the sort of business challenge about which even large corporations think twice before throwing their resources into the fray. Yet Sue Cook, who has gone on to successfully carve an international niche for her company, has done so without benefit of coming from a business background. Indeed, as she herself, admits, "While I've always personally been interested in business, I never set out to start my own company. I didn't even give it a thought, until it seemed to be the logical thing to do ... I'm the kind of person who just gets up and does a thing. I'm not given to sitting around analysing everything."

The daughter of a university professor, Sue undertook a Masters Degree in computing science at Montreal and Quebec. In 1987, she came to Aberdeen University for a year's study to complete her degree, and decided to stay. It would not be overstating matters to say she fell in love with the country. "I liked the culture, which was very different from what I'd been used to," she says. "I found the people to be warm and kind - once I'd got over the 'what the heck are they saying' bit. It took a little while before I got used to the accents."

On completion of her degree, Sue worked briefly in Dubai in the Middle East for a computer company, then returned to Scotland where in 1989 she married Mark, whom she had met at Aberdeen University. Like herself, he had been studying there, his field being bio-chemistry and immunology.

That same year, Sue set up Broad Knowledge Systems to develop multi-media systems for an international market. The Scottish Office, keen for the country to be in on the ground floor of what was a radically new computer technology field, and impressed by Sue's plans, weighed in with a £25,000 innovation award (another award is in the offing to help the company market revolutionary new technology it has developed). That first major injection of capital was an important breakthrough for Broad Knowledge Systems, because of the long lead-in times involved in both in landing contracts and in creating systems for clients.

As Broad Knowledge Systems, Sue's initial role was acting as a technical consultant in computing and project management. With the contacts she had made in Dubai, it wasn't long before she found herself back in the Middle East working on the first multi-media system for the United Arab Emirates Airforce. It was a large and important contract in which her company was required - with other experts in the field - to provide a system which gave dual language information on a wide range of military aircraft, together with data on their capabilities, their technical specifications and the companies which manufactured them.

Working with an associate company, Computer Electronics World, which marketed the project to manufacturers, Broad Knowledge Systems spent 18 months designing an inter-active system which integrated sound, graphics, video, digitised voice, 3D animation and music. All the details in the new computerised data base, which ranged from the historical background of companies to military performance and technical data, were translated into both Arabic and airforce English. In addition, Broad Knowledge Systems also designed the hardware and a specially cooled unit to house the multi-media system - in itself no small task, given that it was being asked to protect delicate electronic components in a climate where extreme temperatures are the norm. The system, known as Comm-Intel (Command Intelligence), was unveiled at the Paris Air Show in 1991, to considerable international acclaim.

Cutting her teeth on that major assignment, which employed many of the multi-media techniques Broad Knowledge Systems was later to adapt for Scottish use in other fields, gave Sue invaluable experience. Regular visits back to Canada - still several years ahead in its applications of multi-media systems - provided not only knowledge about new hardware coming on the market, but also reinforced her belief that she was working in a field set for major expansion.

Back in Scotland, though, marketing the service proved a painfully slow process. It took Sue a full year to land a £20,000 contract with West Lothian District Council, which was considering trying out a multi-media information system to provide people in Livingston with a public information point outlining its council services. Similarly, when Broad Knowledge Systems was contracted by Fife Health Board to undertake the largest public health information programme ever devised in Scotland, again it was 12 months before the Board signed up to a £100,000 deal. To land the business, Sue undertook an intensive marketing campaign which involved Broad Knowledge Systems staging no less than seven on-site demonstrations of what her service could do, physically transporting her equipment up to Fife each time. In fact, "road shows" with demonstration model programmes today play a key part in her sales strategy. "It's a lot easier to demonstrate what inter-active multi-media systems can do than to talk about them," she says. "People think they know what they are, but they really don't. That's why we find it best to physically show them."

Nevertheless, she admits the long lead-in time in landing contracts is the single biggest worry faced by the business. On top of the 12 months "lag time" while the deal ferments has to be added the period required to visualise, script and computerise the specialised information package for the client. That varies in accordance with its complexity, and can take anything from three months to two years.

"There's a huge outlay," Sue says. "But everybody goes through tough times and I keep in my mind where I am going and where I want to be. I hold firmly to the fact that I'm going to get there. We're not selling something that is quick. If you have an expensive product, it takes time. I think every small company which works on a contract basis worries about where the next one is coming from - no matter what field it is in. But I finally feel that I am getting to the top of the hill after a tremendous struggle. Recently people have become more aware of the word, multi-media. When I call someone these days, they think they know what I'm talking about, which overcomes one big hurdle. As more and more people become aware of the advantages of multi-media, it will become easier. Maybe we'll be able to reduce the year negotiating contracts to six months. We're also finding that our clients are talking about us to other people, which is a fabulous development."

During the lean times, while trying to negotiate big contracts, both Sue and her husband have taken on "bread and butter" consultancy work both at home and abroad for a wide variety of organisations, providing information systems. Clients have included hotels, museums, the oil industry and international conferences. Broad Knowledge Systems has conducted computer training and network consultation work from Sri Lanka to London.

The West Lothian contract was a notable Scottish breakthrough for Broad Knowledge Systems, in that it was the company's first local authority project. It took eight months to research and package the information in an interesting format for the council.

On the face of it, £20,000 - which includes the price of providing the £10,000 custom-made public information unit on which the material is accessed - may seem somewhat niggardly reward for a multi-media programme containing the equivalent of 600 "pages" of information. Sue's computerised programme for West Lothian encompasses details on individual council services; information on councillors and the wards they represent; voting qualifications and how to register; and material on environmental health; leisure; tourism and a raft of other related topics. On tap to the public, if they have the stamina for it, is eight hours of continuous viewing. However, in pricing its service, Broad Knowledge Systems was looking very much to the future: When a multi-media company wins a client, it does so long-term, if not for life.

There are annual maintenance contracts for the hardware, software and information dispensing units. These contracts also cover updating information or adding new categories of data to the package. In flexibility, multi-media scores heavily over conventional ways of dispensing information.

Printed literature such as newsletters, or, for that matter, corporate videos, from the moment of completion, are already dated - because they cannot be altered. Nor are they able to get their individual users "talking" back to those trying to reach them with information. Multi-media systems accommodate both facilities.

Built into the information package is a monthly audit which tells the client how many people have accessed the system, their sex, age and what subjects they have looked at. There are also sections which allow the public to state what additional information they would like the system to contain. That invaluable and regular "feedback" means information can be constantly, and easily, "fine tuned" according to the dictates of public demand. Equally, if the client organisation finds that an important message it is trying to get across isn't being accessed by people, then it can substitute it with a different, and better, way of saying it.

In West Lothian that "feedback" facility - or tracking, as it is known - told the council where to site its public information unit for maximum effect. Originally sited at a housing office, monthly audits revealed low usage. Resited in the town centre at a large grocery supermarket, figures rose dramatically. The multi-media tracking system also highlighted a major concern by townspeople over dog fouling which resulted in the council providing the public with free "poop scoops" at a nearby locus. The multi-media system today remains at its current site in Livingston, providing the council with an on-going dialogue with the people it serves. It acts as an electronic council office.

The single most interesting statistic flung up by the tracking system, however, has been the age profile of public accessing Livingston's local authority multi-media system: It reflects no age barriers. Pensioners, who might reasonably be expected to be the generation least comfortable in using new technology, consult it as often as do teenagers. What that demonstrates is that the 'touch screen' approach, which does away with keyboards, coupled with Broad Knowledge Systems' method of multi-media information packaging, has successfully broken down the "fear factor" concerning computer technology. That, alone, represents a hugely significant advance, one which will colour the expansion of multi-media's general usage. The barriers between technology and people are coming down in a way which has never really happened before in Britain.

The Fife Health Board project presented challenges of a different magnitude: How to reach out with health education information to young people aged between 14 and 18. As a peer group, teenagers are notoriously difficult for organisations to talk to effectively on contraception, safe sex, drugs and their effects, HIV, smoking, drinking and other health topics such as diet and nutrition. It is in the way of the world for elders and authorities to proffer advice to youth and for youth to roundly ignore it - whether it be a bright young student going bad on a good education or a 16-year-old school leaver spurning advice in a mixture of rebellion and naiveté. Youth culture, by its very nature, sets out to exclude older generations; it is governed by its own internal set of mores. It may well have a point: It is being asked to listen to advice from generations which gave the world Hiroshima, the Holocaust, Vietnam, the Gulf War, the break-down of the family unit and, in Britain, a highly imperfect social system which has signally failed to give young people the jobs and employment security previously enjoyed by their elders.

These days, after a great deal of trial and error, it has been established that the best way to reach young people is not to "talk down" to them or to try to scare them out of health-endangering social activities, but to present them with the plain, unvarnished facts, the pluses and the negatives, in a non-judgmental, non-partisan way, then let them make up their own minds on issues. If the information can be delivered by someone from within their own age group or to whom they can strongly relate, so much the better.

In Fife, health authorities were concerned about the high incidence of unwanted teenage pregnancies and the youth drugs and drink culture sweeping with frightening speed through Scotland. Realising from the statistics crossing its desk that conventional campaigns were at best being only partially successful, the Health Board decided to make a radical departure from them. Through inter-active multi-media, it set out to establish a permanent two-way link between itself and the county's teenagers. In addition to providing information, it wanted the system to track young people's main worries by age group and sex and to conduct anonymous surveys on users' attitudes to particular topics.

It was a hugely ambitious project, one which involved Broad Knowledge Systems providing some 7000 "pages" of information, the equivalent of eight full days of continuous viewing, on health subjects. In preparing and presenting the information provided by the Board's experts, the company also had to deploy the full range of visual and cinematic techniques to which young people are accustomed. Broad Knowledge Systems became, in effect, the producer and director of an eight-day-long movie. It had never been done in Scotland before.

One of the new factors in its preparation was the employment of a world-beating technology lead which the company had just pioneered through Sue's husband, Mark, who had by now joined Broad Knowledge Systems as its full-time technical director. Although computer technology had not been his university degree course, he had an excellent knowledge of the field and had developed a method of quadrupling the play time of laser discs. Used to provide high resolution pictures which can be expanded in size without loss of quality, the discs normally run for 30 minutes on each side. Mark found a method of compressing information on them which increased the play time to two hours per side - a trail-breaking innovation which the company has now patented, because the development has far-reaching implications for the whole computer technology industry. What the new technological advance did was provide Broad Knowledge Systems with a world exclusive means to produce slicker, more versatile high quality visuals within their health information package.

It took two years for the company to compile and format the information, devising layers of questions and answers which became progressively more detailed the deeper youngsters delved into the subject. To keep on course, and ensure they were correctly tailoring material in a way which engaged teenagers' interest, Broad Knowledge Systems conducted regular interviews with groups of pupils at Kirkcaldy High School, ascertaining the youth viewpoint.

For the Fife Health Board, just as important as providing public information was establishing a dialogue with the county's young people. Broad Knowledge Systems was required to incorporate quite sophisticated tracking methods to elicit responses from teenagers using the system without them being really aware that their attitudes and habits were being sampled. Undoubtedly, there exists a certain "giggle" factor and youthful bravado which can distort the true picture being built up; young people tend to use public information multi-media systems in small groups of four or five, with one person selecting topics from the menu of choices. However, the deeper any user progresses into the system, the greater is the likelihood of that person giving genuine responses. Truth has a habit of asserting itself. The cloak of anonymity, too, is also reckoned to produce more accurate results than conventional sampling. "How many 13-year-olds give truthful answers on youth sexuality when confronted by an adult with a clipboard?" asks Sue.

Broad Knowledge Systems also knows, though, that to some questions getting truthful answers is difficult. "We realise that, in front of their friends crowded round a health information unit, young people are seldom going to admit that they have learned something new about, say drugs or sex. They're going to say they know it all." says Sue. "In reality, though, we know multi-media is either providing them with new information or reinforcing some aspect about which they had forgotten. We also know that young people will come back on their own to follow up on information which is of interest to them."

But one way or another, teenagers' attitudes and, at times naiveté, have a way of shining through. Revelations from the Health Board multi-media system have included statistics which show many young people don't realise they can just say No to sex; others didn't know that there were condoms for women or that alcohol was a drug. Armed with that type of data, Fife Health Board is now better placed than any health authority in Scotland to adapt its health education information and to launch new campaigns which address specific issues and fill in gaps in teenagers' knowledge.

The delivery systems for public multi-media programmes also play an important role in how effectively information is dispensed. There are certain obvious factors such as location and ensuring they are vandal-proof. The touch screens are made of a specially toughened material, and the housing which encloses the electronic components is also of a highly durable nature. But there are more subtle considerations, too. Every unit is equipped with quick exit buttons to spare people any embarrassment if discovered accessing medical information. "If you're out shopping with your granny you don't want her to see you asking the computer if you have a sexually transmitted disease," says Sue.

To handle the workload in developing Fife's health information system, and other contracts, Broad Knowledge Systems has had to staff up. Sue now employs four full-time staff, a secretary, a graphics designer and a programmer. With space at a premium, she expects to have to relocate within Edinburgh as the business continues to expand.

Having established a proven and sophisticated framework, on which it can base other multi-media systems, the company is now targeting local authorities for other contracts in the field of public information or training. Sue likens it to establishing a picture gallery, in which her business has put up all the hooks. "All we need to do now is change the pictures," she says.

That is perhaps an over-simplification. But there is no doubt that as the first multi-media company in Scotland, Broad Knowledge Systems has established a commanding lead over rival companies coming into the field. "We've been around since 1989. Most of them started arriving about a year ago," says Sue.

As a Canadian who has now become an adopted Scot, she is very aware of one very one considerable cultural difference in the way the two countries do business. In Scotland, businesses play their cards very close to their chest.

There is not the same level of exchange in commercial information between companies. She says: "In Canada, companies help each other out, even if they are working in the same line. They reckon there is always going to be enough business around for everyone. But that doesn't happen here. Everybody is very secretive."

It is one of the reasons she is a founder member of a new organisation, the Inter-active Media Alliance Scotland, where multi-media companies can meet to exchange information about their fledgling industry which is about to blossom into a massive international commercial sector in the early part of the 21st century. Broad Knowledge Systems is a company aptly named.

CHAPTER FIVE

Cuts service that's tough at the top

IF YOU have ever wondered what the first task of the day is for the bosses of our biggest companies when they arrive in the office, let me enlighten you: It is keeping themselves informed. Every morning across Britain, usually between 8 and 8.30am, the top decision makers in a wide array of organisations in both the public and private sector spend 15 to 20 minutes rapidly scanning specially prepared digests of what Britain's national and regional daily papers contain.

Irrespective of their sphere of business interests, that level of awareness is vital to them all. Finance, industry, investment and commerce do not happen in a vacuum. Their performances are directly affected by whatever else is going on in the world. As well as following events and trends within their own specialist fields, leaders of major organisations and their various business divisions need to know about general news events. They have to "hit the deck running."

To cite one small, hypothetical example: If a council tries to curb outbreaks of public disorder and street violence by deciding to press for a 12-month curfew on city centre night life, the commercial ripples of such a decision extend well beyond the clubs, pubs and discos being ordered to close early. The drinks industry is obviously affected. But the curfew might just as easily penalise the tourist trade, taxis and hotels, or torpedo an important city centre leisure project which a developer is trying to push ahead. Equally it might jeopardise a closely fought battle by Local and Central Government agencies against rivals to "capture" a prestigious business conference or a big inward investment project. Forewarned is forearmed. The unexpected threat may require to be countered immediately by some form of direct intervention, such as mobilising opposition to the plan through statements to the media, or through a trade organisation. At the very least, immediate soundings have to be taken by businesses and other agencies to assess its potential ramifications.

Thus before being swept up in the heavy workload of normal company affairs, decision makers jealously preserve a slot in their work schedule during which they can assimilate quickly the main general news of the day, together with the principal stories in their own field. Senior executives know that the specially compiled press packages are a fast, efficient method of bringing themselves up to speed. In a few minutes they can read the equivalent of up to a dozen different newspapers, stripped down to main stories and commentaries.

News digests are also required reading for leaders of key departments in public bodies. They have to be aware of political nuances or potential shifts in Government thinking which could affect how they carry out their functions; they also have to keep abreast of public opinion on a wide range of issues. Property development, for example, often requires sensitive handling. The needs and anxieties of the wider community have to be taken into account. It is important to maintain the "feel good" factor when creating, say, a new business park in a suburban location. Business investment is largely based upon confidence; too much adverse comment or controversy surrounding our mythical business park, and occupancy rates could be seriously lowered. In turn, that could affect both its financial success and the valuable commercial spin-offs it is supposed to trigger within a community.

Every day, therefore, rather like the Mississippi river captains of old, professional executives of public bodies have to check whether the sand bars have shifted and the waters are shoaling- then adjust the wheel a few points to circumvent the danger.

Their political masters are engaged in much the same exercise.

For Scottish Government Ministers, who spend much of their time in London, the daily collation of photostat clippings from the Scottish press, plus a breakdown of how many papers carried particular news items, is a quite vital link. Flipping through anything up to 100 pages of news items, important features, selected editorial comment and perhaps even a number of Letters to the Editor, they can absorb the mood of the country on a host of issues. Having taken the nation's pulse each morning, Ministers react as required to any political situation which calls for their immediate attention.

If an executive or politician, used to having an 8am news digest on his desk as he hangs up his jacket, doesn't see it appear by 8.04, by 8.05 he will be on the phone to his subordinates demanding to know what has happened to it. The reality is that, without it, he feels he is facing the world naked.

Amid the plethora of electronic information technology available, it may seem odd that many of the big business and political decisions directly affecting our lives should stem, in part, from reactions to a service which relies on old-fashioned "scissors and paste" methodology. Its apparent simplicity, though, is deceptive. Running a good quality cuttings agency is labour-intensive, exacting work where deadlines are tight and the margin for error (in terms of missed stories) is slim. It is arguably one of the toughest service industries around.

One of the largest, and growing, agencies in Scotland is the Press Data Bureau in Edinburgh. Founded nearly five years ago by Jerry Ward, aged 30, it today employs 11 full-time researchers to service more than 40 major clients. Companies on its books include five of the top ten businesses in Scotland. From its office premises off Rose Street, in Edinburgh city centre, the company is also making promising inroads into the English market place, picking up new clients in both London and along the English south coast.

At first glance, Jerry's background makes him an unlikely candidate to handle such a business venture. The son of a buyer for a paper company, he was born and brought up in South London as one of a family of four children. Very much against the trends of the time, his father when in his early forties surprisingly forsook his safe staff job to strike out on an entirely new career. He and a print sales rep joined forces to set up a small printer's business. "He wasn't made redundant or anything," said Jerry. "This was the mid-sixties and it was very rare for someone of his age to move out of a staff job to become self-employed. But he was an intelligent man, and probably realised this was probably his last chance to do what he wanted to do. My mother wasn't keen at all; the pressure was on him not to start the business. It was never wholly successful but he did quite well out of it and retired in his mid-fifties."

Although the ethos within the family was very much one of self-sufficiency, there appeared to be no prospect of Jerry following in his father's footsteps. His interests lay in an entirely different direction; he wanted to work in films. In 1984 Jerry moved to Scotland, where, over five years, he took a four-year course in film and media studies at Stirling University. He emerged from the course with a Bachelor of Arts degree, and a deep desire to make his home -

and his living - in Scotland. The latter proved impossible. Advancing his career in any meaningful way meant moving South. As Jerry, himself, admits, "I'd done a very interesting degree but I was pretty unemployable. I didn't have much experience and I wanted to stay in Scotland. I tried for television and TV-related work without having to go to London - but those two things were incompatible."

For a full year Jerry manfully tried to square the circle, taking on a variety of jobs on Scottish productions, working for nothing just to get the experience. Over the 12 months he was employed variously as a runner, general dogsbody and researcher on a number of projects - all unpaid. It got him precisely nowhere. By 1990, deeply disillusioned and broke, he took the first job he could get, which happened to be with a media monitoring company in Edinburgh. To his astonishment, he discovered he had "lucked" into a job he loved. Having concentrated so heavily on a film industry career, Jerry had all but forgotten what the print side of the media had to offer. Immersed in monitoring its stories, he found it utterly fascinating.

For 18 months, Jerry remained with the agency learning the business. Once he had mastered his duties, and still bubbling with enthusiasm, he bombarded its head office in London with ideas on how to increase the company's Scottish customer base, and take advantage of opportunities which he saw cropping up. A Londoner himself, for the first time he came up against the highly frustrating "North of Watford" barrier. Head office simply wasn't interested. It viewed its Scottish operation merely as an adjunct to its London service, existing solely as a clearing house to feed important Scottish commercial news down the line to be sent out to its London customers. Building up a Scottish client base wasn't in the scheme of things. Despite the high calibre of staff in the Edinburgh office, it was regarded as a provincial backwater. Jerry quickly realised that any promotional route within the company lay in London.

Once again, to further personal career aspirations, he was confronted with the unpalatable prospect of having to return South. Once again, it was an option he rejected. While still with the company, he began to work out the costs of going it alone and forming his own agency. He also researched lists of Scottish companies which might have a need for his services.

In the event, though, it was a personal business contact who was to launch him on his new career. He broached the subject with a business friend within a Scottish bank, saying he was thinking of starting up an agency: Would the bank consider taking his service? Word came back that it would. That was enough for Jerry. Borrowing £1000 from his father, and with one prospective client, he bought himself a photo-copier, a desk, a fax machine and a typewriter, all second hand, installed them in the bedroom of his flat, and started up.

It was a rough beginning. For six months his sole client was the bank. The cash he earned supplying its head office with a daily cuttings service didn't even begin to look at his overheads; a cuttings service, like a newspaper syndication department, needs numerous customers to make its services profitable. Doggedly Jerry went about trying to grow the business, spending every available minute compiling sales pitches and marketing his service round scores of companies. There were mail drops and personal follow ups of any leads. He spoke to anyone who would listen but nobody was very interested in what he had to offer. And a lot of doubts were beginning to assail the fledgling entrepreneur.

From his own knowledge, he knew the rates he was offering were pitched well within service norms. They were neither over nor under-priced, being in the mainstream of charges made by other cuttings agencies. Price was not a barrier to progress. Yet the business wasn't coming in. He began asking himself some serious questions. Could it be that as a sole trader he was too vulnerable? Were companies afraid they would be left without a service if he went out of business?

As if in direct answer to those questions, his sole client suddenly cancelled. There was no complaint about the quality of service being provided. The bank pulled out because, it said, the Press Data Bureau's continued existence was too problematical; it wanted to take a service from a company it knew would always be there. The bank switched to Jerry's former company in Edinburgh.

In one of those supreme ironies worthy of Denis Norden's "It'll Be All Right On The Night" TV programmes, two weeks later the bank suffered precisely the fate it had sought to avoid. Jerry's old company terminated the new contract because its Scottish office was being wound up.

As a private Robert Maxwell company, following the controversial newspaper tycoon's mysterious death by drowning when he vanished from his company yacht while sailing in the Canaries, it had found itself caught up in the monstrous financial morass he left behind. Accountants called in to assess the true worth of every company owned by the erstwhile Daily Mirror proprietor very quickly established that the London media information bureau's Scottish office was a luxury it couldn't afford. Because it had not been permitted to develop its own range of Scottish clients (as Jerry had suggested), it was not a revenue earner but a company liability. They closed it down.

Composing a suitable poker face, Jerry sympathised with the bank's dilemma and offered to reinstate his service, this time at his normal rates, which were higher than his original cut-price deal, saying: "I am going to stick around; I am not going away - and I can give you a better service than you got from London."

The bank turned him down. Even now, though the Press Data Bureau is firmly established as a soundly profitable business, the bank still prefers to take its service from elsewhere. For an outside company, being in close proximity to the Emperor when he is embarrassingly disclosed as having no clothes, is a distinctly long-term trading disadvantage. It is a question of loss of face.

For almost three months after the bank pulled out, Jerry had no customers whatsoever. At around this juncture, most entrepreneurs might well have cut their losses, shut up shop and gone on to try something else. What kept Jerry going, apart from his natural tenacity, was the hope of landing a contract with Scottish Enterprise, the then recently created organisation which had replaced the Scottish Development Agency. Funded by Central Government, Scottish Enterprise was - and is - Scotland's principal domestic investment powerhouse. It is tasked with the job of modernising the country's infra-structure and being the catalyst of new industrial opportunity through investment, training and a multiplicity of business and commercial initiatives. It is also charged with the role of fostering a new, more confident entrepreneurial spirit within Scotland.

In commerce, as in life, timing is all. In canvassing for business, Jerry Ward had had the good fortune to encounter Scottish Enterprise's chief executive, Gerry O'Brien, at just the right juncture. He expressed great interest in Jerry's company, because one of Scottish Enterprise's more pressing needs, as a young and evolving organisation, was a source of continuous feedback on what the Press was reporting about its operations.

Although today Scottish Enterprise enjoys a very considerable degree of public awareness, support and confidence right across the full spectrum of Scottish life, things were rather different at its inception. Its formation had not been without political controversy. At the time the Press Data Bureau came on the scene, Scottish Enterprise, over and above the task of kick-starting the Scottish economy, was still engaged in a "hearts and minds" exercise to establish its credentials. That meant leading from the front with considerable energy, heavily publicising and promoting its numerous initiatives. Having a "sounding board" which reflected back public opinion was highly necessary to establish how effectively it was getting across its message.

It took three months, though, for Jerry Ward to convince Scottish Enterprise that the Press Data Bureau could deliver the type of service the organisation needed. Within weeks of clinching the deal, Jerry also landed a second contract, this time with insurance giant Standard Life. From being on the verge of extinction, the Press Data Bureau was at long last on its way. As the business began to expand Jerry moved out of his flat into proper premises.

Looking back on those tense opening months, Jerry enumerates some of the lessons he learned the hard way. Two concern his marketing strategies. In the beginning, he used to send out one standard information pack to businesses. Today all promotional material to a potential client is customer-specific. "I used to send out a generalised pack of what I could supply and it was met with deafening silence," he says. "People couldn't relate it directly to their own business needs. Now when I send out sample packs they contain precisely the information we will be supplying that company with, if they sign up. We get a much better response from that approach because companies immediately see its relevance to their own business operations."

Targeting firms also had to be refined. In seeking contracts, very early on Jerry discovered that the most important factor was not company size, but where the decisions were made. If the company had a London HQ, or if its public relations firm was London-based, the chances of getting it to take on board a Scottish cuttings agency were negligible, even though the organisation might have very considerable commercial interests in Scotland. Before targeting a company, therefore, Jerry had to do his homework. Not only had he to establish its command structure, he also had to research in some detail the way individual companies worked.

"It was a very steep learning curve," he confesses. "Originally I thought I could offer a generic service to companies in the same business sectors but I very quickly discovered that, even within the same field, businesses often operated in fundamentally different ways. It was impossible to generalise. They all had their special needs ... My marketing today is still very much a lobbying process, letting people know we're here. My sales technique concentrates on building relations with companies rather than just selling them something. After all, we are supplying them with a special service every day."

In the beginning, though, Jerry encountered a great deal of business scepticism. He says: "Some people were receptive to ideas and would give you a meeting. They would hear you out, even if they didn't buy. But mostly, people were very cautious. Today that culture has changed. I certainly feel companies are more receptive. A lot of that, I think, is down to us now having a very strong client base. When they see the list, companies know they have to take me seriously."

That the Press Data Bureau is taken seriously these days, there is no doubt. Recently it was one of two companies chosen by the Scottish Office to supply it with a complete daily cuttings service from Scotland on a six-month trial basis, and in March was awarded the contract - a business coup of considerable magnitude. It is the first time that the Scottish Office has allowed the job of compiling daily media information for its needs to be carried out externally. Every morning the Bureau begins transmission of material to the Scottish Office around 6.30am. The physical act of just faxing it over takes an hour.

To service all its clients, the Press Data Bureau has to run its operation like a slickly professional daily newspaper. It has to be fast and accurate, and its deadlines are as tight as any evening paper striving to get out its first edition. For Jerry and his staff the day begins at 5.30am - the earliest they can obtain the morning newspapers. Within minutes titles are being read and cut by teams of researchers, all of whom are university graduates. The material is then funnelled through the Production Manager, who acts as a News Editor. It is his job to decide the editorial content which will be sent out to individual companies in their customised daily packs.

Most of the news items allocate themselves, because the researchers all have their own list of companies, whose needs they know intimately. They also monitor their own clients' packs. However, inevitably there are "marginal" business or financial stories on which the Production Manager adjudicates. That quality control on selection of information is essential: If it is too indiscriminate it defeats the object of the exercise, which is to supply sharply honed information; too narrow a spectrum of news coverage and it might miss items of importance. Notwithstanding the selection process, in the course of a day literally hundreds of stories are cut and distributed to clients from something like 30 national and regional titles.

By 6.15am some of the readers begin to peel off to start the process of production and packaging of information, while the remainder continue to scan newspapers and any late arrival editions for other articles which will be slotted into packs on a running basis. All the material selected is scanned directly into the Bureau's computer system, and the individual news packages collated and faxed over to clients. In some instances hard copies are couriered round to their offices.

"Our service goes directly to the top," says Jerry. "The material is read by chief executives and at director level. It comes in the door and within 30 seconds it is on the boss's desk. You are delivering straight to the top, and you just can't be late. Everyone is looking for the daily digest between 8.00 to 8.30am. With the Scottish Office it has to be over by 7.30am because there is so much material to fax. Between 6.30am and 7am they are looking for 60 to 100 pages of information."

There is little or no room for error in the operation. Hiccups like late delivery of certain titles because of distribution problems, which can occur two or three times a month, have to be taken in their stride. "We have to adapt if that happens, but even on bad days we usually can manage to get most titles by 8.30am," says Jerry. "It's a tough job and there are no passengers. Everyone works under great pressure. Staff here work a 30-hour week because doing a full 8-hour shift pushes you into the realm of making mistakes through tiredness; this is a job which requires a lot of heavy, high speed concentration."

Against that backdrop, appointing staff of the right calibre is crucial, which is why Jerry employs only university graduates. He says: "All our readers are educated to degree level. That's not prejudice on our part. It's simply that the research disciplines employed in gaining a degree are the same sort of skills we require here. There is a need for attention to detail, and an ability to read and digest information. We need people who can do that, then make informed judgements."

The discipline of the job calls for fairly ruthless efficiency. New staff operate under the wing of more experienced colleagues as they are trained. But if they fail to make the grade they are paid off on the spot and replaced. "I've had to sack people instantly," says Jerry. "One bad researcher means you are permanently a person down because their judgement can't be trusted. One miss on, say, an important financial story could cost us a client. Our customers are loyal, but they are only loyal because we provide a first class service. A poor researcher is a real danger to us."

To ensure everyone stays on top of the job, the company holds regular briefings with both its clients and its own researchers. Jerry says: "We're involved in a fairly sophisticated process. In the first instance, we meet with customers, and identify what they need and how to get it to them. We then train our researchers on how to fill those needs. We issue briefing documents, and hold regular staff meetings when client information comes through. Researchers also make up their own personal files and notes on clients. They become experienced in finding out associated subjects in which the companies may be interested; in fact, sometimes they are more knowledgeable than the clients, themselves, on their needs."

The toughest sector for which to get top-class researchers, says Jerry, is finance, particularly lifestyle and personal finance. "It's a very complicated sector - there is just so much of it. It's also the area where there are the least numbers of skilled people available. We have to specially train everyone who covers it."

If internal staffing is tough, the external commercial pressures on Jerry's business are even tougher. His policy of gradualism in growing the business and expanding services is immediately understandable when weighed against the contracts system under which he has to operate. Nothing is long-term. In the public sector, contracts of 6 to 12 months' duration are the norm. Within the private sector, the maximum length of contract is usually three months. Indeed, week-to-week contracts are not unknown.

Given the amount of care and time his company devotes to clients, "fine-tuning" its service to their needs, Jerry very rightly refuses to get into the realm of the seven-day contracts taken on by some of his rivals. Nevertheless, his bargaining power on length of contracts is heavily constrained by the general practices of his industry. In costing his service, he finds it impossible to introduce a tariff system which would encourage companies to take on lengthier agreements. He relies on quality of service to retain customer loyalty. "Right from the start my aim was to offer a high quality service," he says. "I'm not interested in offering anything else. If I found I was being forced to compromise on excellence, I wouldn't want to be in this business; I'd be off doing something else."

That personal commitment to quality also makes sound business sense. It is one of life's truisms that companies are seldom happy with their cuttings agencies. Simmering beneath the surface is a resentment factor that they have to use them at all; that hidden irritation is reinforced and bubbles up every time an agency fails to deliver a particular news item or company profile which has appeared in the Press. It is grossly unfair, but it is a fact of life. Jerry has lost track of the number of social gatherings he has attended where company executives, on hearing what he does, have drawn him aside to tell him they want to change to another agency.

Usually there is not a great deal of logic involved in the desire for change, save a vague discontent and a feeling that, somehow, the organisation isn't getting value for money. Yet the logistics speak for themselves: For a company to devote its own staff to media monitoring isn't cost-effective. Using a professional cuttings agency like the Press Data Bureau means that, for a fraction of the cost of employing a full-time staff member on the job, it has access to almost a dozen highly experienced researchers, who are experts in numerous fields.

No matter how positive a feedback Jerry gets from clients, he never forgets that in the world of the cuttings agencies, client loyalty can never be taken for granted.

The Next Generation

As if pressure deadlines, short-term contracts and latent prejudice against the industry is not enough to contend with, Jerry faces another major hurdle: The explosion of information technology going on around him. International news agencies, newspaper groups and specialist directory publishers have all invaded the commercial information services sector in a big way. A truly formidable array of material, from teletext services to on-line specialist information, is now available. The electronic newspaper is already with us.

Faced with the necessity of having to adapt to meet changing trading conditions, Jerry is also confronted by a bewildering range of electronic choices. Information technology and constant innovation have opened up an incredible variety of options. Inevitably, many of them will prove to be commercial dead ends. To keep abreast of the field, Jerry now has a researcher whose specialist subject is information technology and its new applications. "I don't have any magical answer," he says. "I'd like to think I am responsive enough to make the right decisions when those decisions have to be made - and, yes, thinking about it does make me break out in cold sweats now and again. That is why right now we are closely monitoring developments."

In the meantime, Jerry continues to cast around for new outlets for his services. Currently being targeted in Scotland are the country's local authorities, and south of the border he is trying to develop more clients in and around London. "We couldn't do it a couple of years ago, but we now have the resources to expand our services," he says.

On the horizon, too, dependent upon the outcome of the next General Election, is the possibility of a Scottish Parliament being established in Edinburgh. If that ever comes to fruition, a new opportunity arises to supply politicians and the Secretariat with a special "fast read" Parliamentary news digest of what Scottish newspapers are reporting. The Bureau is one of the few companies around which has both the resources and the organisation to provide such a service.

That type of development lies very much in a problematic future. For today, Jerry is happy to grow his business along conventional lines, while keeping a weather eye open on the changing technological climate. He enjoys the work and is confident that the business will continue to evolve and expand. But don't let anyone tell you it is easy. On balance, it is probably one of the hardest niche businesses in Scotland, and certainly, within its customer base, the most unforgiving of mistakes.

CHAPTER SIX

Flower power exudes confidence

IN business, appearance counts. We equate it with efficiency. When we walk into the reception area of a company which through its decor projects an attractive, confident image of itself to the outside world, it inspires within us - if only subconsciously - a belief that here is an organisation which knows what it is doing. About the only time this fails to comfort us is when we pass through the portals of a top lawyer's office and wonder how much of our fees go to support the limited edition prints on the wall and the char lady so industriously polishing up the brasses.

A relatively cheap method of achieving that prosperous-looking corporate appearance is through the installation of displays of plants and flowers. Scottish business - perhaps because of our less favourable climate - has been slower to appreciate the effectiveness of massed plants in office displays than the rest of Europe, where even the meanest trattoria is routinely transformed into a magical place by their use. But when commerce eventually did catch on to plant displays' ability to brighten up offices, saying it with flowers became big business. These days it is a niche market commanding a United Kingdom spend estimated at nearly £50 million, with an annual growth rate of about 10 per cent. In the jargon of the times it now often is known as interior landscaping.

Apart from their clean, "green" image and decorative value, there are sound environmental reasons for the use of plant displays in offices. Plants help scrub the air clean of the small quantities of pollutants emitted by office equipment such as photo-copiers, new carpeting, polish, veneers, plastics and many other materials. Many of these trace toxins are absorbed through the leaves, eventually being converted to food. As a by-product, plants also enrich the indoor oxygen supply. They are also reputed to reduce stress levels among staff. Thus in banks, hotels, leisure centres, restaurants and museums, indeed any building in regular commercial use, they are a useful addition to business surroundings. As well as having to be knowledgeably installed, they also require to be maintained on a regular basis, which is why interior landscaping has flowered as a fully fledged floral commercial service in its own right.

Currently making a great success of her entry into the industry in Scotland is 27-year-old Belinda Jarron, with her award-winning company, Fleurtations. It is worthy of examination on a number of fronts. These include Belinda's extremely clear vision in mapping out her career from university onwards; her ability as a young boss to command the support and enthusiasm of employees a good deal older than herself; and the major marketing challenges she is still resolving.

Fleurtations is based in a small industrial estate in the one-time mining village of Wallyford, near Edinburgh. Within a factory unit where her parents manufacture gear wheels for industry, Belinda occupies a small section of the open-plan office for her business, although she has a storage workshop area elsewhere to accommodate equipment, pot plants and other paraphernalia of her trade.

Given her family's business background, it is perhaps not surprising that from the outset Belinda has always known she would be working for herself and founding her own company. Educated at North Berwick High School, she went on to Bath University, where she followed up a life-long interest in plants and flowers by taking a four-year B Sc Honours degree in horticulture.

Even then, she was planning ahead - tailoring her studies very much to the business she wished to create. In her first year as a student, her placement for practical experience was not overly successful; it was a six-month stint as part of an eight-strong squad, mowing the grass for Edinburgh University. Petite and slightly built Belinda recalls with feeling: "Boy, were those mowers heavy!"

The following year, though, she was successful in gaining a placement with an interior landscaping company in London. For Belinda, it was superb experience. She soaked up knowledge on the firm's operation like a sponge. It was a highly profitable company; nevertheless Belinda also noted its deficiencies. In its day to day running, it failed to keep track of staff; it constantly over-estimated the time it took to carry out contracts, with staff often being able to finish the day's work by lunch-time and head off home - Belinda included. That inefficiency was marked down by Belinda as something to avoid whenever she founded her own business.

That day, though, was still some way off. To escape having to study crop growing at Bath as part of her degree course, Belinda went to the USA to continue horticultural studies at the University of Maryland, where she obtained a Merit in Landscape Architecture. Back at Bath, for her thesis, she was able to devote it to what was in essence valuable marketing research into her chosen field. On completion of her degree at Bath, although it delayed by a year her plans to set up in business for herself, she went on to Cambridge University to take a Master of Philosophy degree in Land Economy. Part of it was the pure challenge of making it to Cambridge (in the face of colleagues who said she was unlikely to be accepted); part of it was as insurance that she would have a career alternative. "I thought I'd better get something else behind me, just in case things went wrong," she says. "A Cambridge degree was a passport to other employment."

In 1991, Fleurtations was born. Belinda, shortly before founding the business, already had acquired one contract. She won it on price, although there was a considerable degree of business naiveté involved; she forgot to include a profit margin for herself in her quote. On the plants side, though, university-educated green fingers prevented Belinda from making mistakes. On early Fleurtations contracts, she knew which plants to instal after personally checking every proposed office location (the commonest being the reception area, the Managing Director's office and the company Boardroom).

"You've got to put the right plants in offices in the first place, otherwise you keep having to change them," she says. "The biggest problem is light. There has got to be enough for plants to survive. What you generally find is if human beings are happy, plants are happy. But if the secretary is cold and chittering and she's got an angle-poise light, plants don't do too well ... I did make the occasional mistake in the first couple of years; I once put in variegated plants in a reception area, forgetting that the company closed the front door AND put out all the lights at weekends."

Other problems encountered had more to do with human nature than office surroundings. Belinda very quickly learned not to site plants next to tea or coffee stations because people kept emptying their cup dregs into them. "When that happens, within months there are bugs in the compost, attracted by the sugar, and any discarded milk goes off," she says. "You can put up notices asking staff not to empty cups into the plant holders, but it's a lot simpler just to avoid the problem altogether by siting the plants somewhere else."

For nearly nine months, Belinda worked from home on her own, putting in 12 hours a day, seven days a week. "I did everything myself. I did the selling; I bought the plants; I put them in; I did the maintenance; kept the books and records. I was putting in huge numbers of hours. Eventually I decided I had to get a life as well," she says.

Belinda moved into her parent's factory unit and began taking on staff to help her. That embroiled her in a whole new set of challenges, the most notable being staff management of people older than herself and how to pass on the knowledge she had absorbed on plant care to others.

Belinda had years of horticultural knowledge at her fingertips. She very quickly could divine the cause of a plant not thriving, and virtually without being aware of it, knew numerous tricks of the trade to improve matters. Successfully passing on that information wasn't always as easy as it looked. When other staff started maintaining the plants, replacement ratios started to become unacceptably high.

To standardise the quality of plant maintenance on service contracts with firms, the Fleurtations staff - who today number three - were issued with a 10-point servicing chart, which they were required to carry out on every display on their round. It was less than successful. On her inspection tours of customers (she covers one-third of her clients every month), Belinda was finding that the displays were of variable standard. Telling staff, two of whom were ten to fifteen years older than the boss, that the ten-point check-list wasn't always being carried out properly proved to be a source of recurring resentment.

There was a second flashpoint area, also. Mindful of her own London experience, Belinda had introduced a slips system detailing how long staff spent on maintenance duties at each firm. The client was required to fill in the times of arrival and departure, sign it, keep the top copy and give the staff the yellow second slip, which was returned to Belinda for entry into her client computer files. Like the inspections, the slips system proved a great bone of contention; staff felt it was an unwarranted checking up on them. But Belinda was unrepentant; the time sheets existed principally for her to keep a continuous check that the business was cost-effectively servicing its contracts. "I budget for six minutes per plant. That's really quite a long time to prune every leaf that is withered; ensure every edge is cut and remove every plant that should be removed; and to dust and spray," she says. "If we are spending too long with one client and not long enough with another, we should know it.

The slips information is put in along with our hourly rate, our plant costs and replacements costs. What the records tell me is whether as a business we are keeping to our correct profit margins. It's an early warning system to ensure every contract is in profit."

To clear the air, Belinda held a staff quality control meeting. At it, she employed a little psychology. Instead of telling them what she wanted, she asked the girls what they would look for if they were promoted to quality control. The suggestions came back thick and fast. Belinda then explained the reasons behind the check list she had devised and the time slips. The success of the meeting prompted her to organise a monthly staff meeting. The first - and, as it transpired, the last - ended in chaos. "I was the only one there at noon, the appointed time. People came wandering in up to an hour late and I went ballistic. Then somebody left, saying they weren't going to be spoken to like that," she recalls. "Afterwards I thought, 'Well, that wasn't a very successful meeting.'We don't have them now. What's the point in storing up grouses for a month? If anyone has a point to make they just raise it with me right away. The girls and I have had our moments in the past, and I've been told a few home truths, but we've sorted things out .. it's a very open style of management."

Tellingly, Belinda's operation has been good enough for her to acquire two of her staff from a rival company, which she admits was a Godsend, saving her the normal six-month training period she reckons is needed for staff who join without previous experience.

For Belinda, systemising her business methods wherever possible has always been a watchword, whether it be the creation of a staff manual or call sheet rotas which show everyone's daily service runs. One of the most practical successes has been establishing a card index file for every client. The cards detail the names of the firm contacts and any relevant details about them; a 'local knowledge' route of how to get there; what the displays are to contain and where they are located in the organisation's building. "Clients are paying us all the year round. They don't want someone coming in and asking, 'Where are your plants?' That's not professional. We have to try and give a professional service at all times," says Belinda. "The client cards mean that on holidays or in cases of illness, anyone can make the visits and know exactly what is required."

Corporate identity is also important for the young entrepreneur. From very early on, Fleurtations has had its own company livery; its fleet of vehicles are all sprayed an eye-catching shocking pink, with the company logo and name picked out in green. Everyone, including Belinda, also wears a smart staff uniform of green and pink, which Belinda designed herself, or in warmer weather, a pink T-shirt. "Sometimes I think, 'What a cheek ... who are you to be designing company logos and uniforms,' " she says. "But in a way we are selling a design service, so we should look the part."

There are fringe benefits to having a clear corporate look, as well. Because of the distinctive uniforms, clients are always aware when Fleurtations staff are in the building, tending displays. Their presence is noticed - always a big psychological plus when dealing in maintenance contracts. "Customers are very loyal. We've never lost a contract to anyone else, once we've won it," says Belinda. "I think it's because when we're in the office, they see us working. They know what they're getting for their money."

Today, Fleurtations numbers several leading Scottish companies on its books, ranging from international plc Kwik-Fit (whose Edinburgh HQ is decorated by the company) to the nuclear power station at Torness. Over the last four years, the company has enjoyed steady growth. Its current turn-over is in excess of £100,000, a 26 per cent increase on the previous year. That is a very creditable achievement in the face of a fairly unrelenting depression across the UK, but Belinda says simply: "In my business life, I have known no business conditions other than depression. Fleurtations was started during an economic downturn and we have still grown. We'll be here for the better times, too."

That confident approach, along the way, has seen Belinda's company voted the best business start-up in her area of Scotland, and she went on to become runner-up in the national final. She spent her prize of £1000 decorating her own personal business car in the company colours.

There have been occasions, though, when Belinda has slightly over-reached herself in her ambition to achieve growth and innovation. The most salutary lesson occurred when she had been in business a little more than two years. With a major contract coming up for fulfilment, she decided to purchase her plants direct from Holland and import them herself.

For Belinda, the Dutch trip was both a fact-finding exercise and an adventure, and before embarking upon it, she had carefully costed it out. Given the size of the upcoming contract, she had calculated the direct bulk buy would pay for itself, plus more than cover the air fares involved, and the expense of freighting the consignment back to Scotland. It was a heady experience for the young businesswoman, strolling through Europe's largest flower auction, into which a truly amazing volume of plants, flowers, bulbs and seeds from all over Germany and Italy are funnelled every week to join the Dutch's own huge horticultural output. Amid the size, colour and apparent confusion of the giant market, Belinda acquitted herself well, picking out the full range of plants she wanted at excellent prices and paid for them, cash on the nail, before arranging for a carrier to bring the consignment to Scotland.

She flew back to Scotland, well satisfied, and filled with dreams of by-passing Scottish wholesalers to become a regular importer from Holland. Cold reality, however, soon intruded. With the big contract deadline fast approaching, and three full days set aside for staff to set up the displays, the plants had not arrived. When they did eventually make an appearance, several days late, there was another body blow. The consignment of large plants destined to be the centre-pieces of the displays were all broken, their stems and leaves snapped in transit. Being perishable goods, they were not insured. All ideas of importing plants by the lorry-load rapidly evaporated. For Belinda it became a race against time, sourcing replacements from Scottish suppliers and getting the displays installed in time for the client.

However, from the wreckage of her Dutch trip, Belinda was able to salvage enough to break even on what should have been a lucrative contract. The smaller plants proved to be undamaged, and by careful trimming she managed to save many of the broken plants as smaller versions for later use. She also refused to pay for the freighting. It was a fraught, nerve-racking episode, one which taught Belinda how easily disrupted her business could be if she expanded her operations prematurely to embrace regular direct imports. The main flaw probably lay in the fact that hers had not been a full load, but a "bit" order filling only about one-third of a container. That probably pushed it down the queue in terms of priority. The rough handling probably stemmed, too, from the fact that it was part of a mixed load. Direct import may well be a route Fleurtations will go down eventually, but only after the company has grown considerably in size, so that consignments ordered are large enough to completely fill containers on their own. In terms of bulk transportation, only might is right. Part cargoes for several delivery destinations get short shrift, save from specialist hauliers.

The drive to source materials at a lower cost without compromising on quality, for all companies, is a constant imperative. Competition breeds cost-saving. For a young company like Fleurtations, at its present stage of development, that route is not really feasible. Lacking the financial muscle to provide it with sufficient safeguards to go it alone and import materials direct from the continent, it is forced to use middlemen, a state of affairs which offers extremely limited scope in cost-cutting. In what is a highly competitive market, the onus for success shifts inexorably to the twin prongs of pricing and marketing. It is here that Belinda faces her greatest company challenge.

With two very major players in the field of interior landscaping in Scotland and about ten other companies of equivalent size to Fleurtations all vying for business, there is little leeway on how companies structure their price lists. How they market themselves to potential clients is therefore crucially important.

To attract as wide as possible a base of clients, most of whom lie in the Central Belt, Belinda has gone for flexibility. Customers can buy outright the displays designed for them, then have their own organisation undertake the maintenance (an option not recommended by Fleurtations on the grounds that staff eventually forget to look after them); they can purchase the displays outright and arrange a maintenance programme with Fleurtations; or they can have purchase and maintenance rolled into a single rental - usually calculated on the basis of entering into a two-year contract. Belinda says the company has contracts which range from as little as £6.50 a month to well over £500, depending on the size of displays. And she expects to make money on them all. The firm's largest single contract is worth around £20,000 per annum.

Contract customers get a fortnightly maintenance visit in which all plants are cleaned and tended, and replacements brought in where necessary. The under-plant foliage is also replaced once a year. Feature plants are renewed usually after three years - or earlier if necessary. "We don't change plants just for the sake of changing them," says Belinda. "We only replace healthy plants if it is required to maintain the right balance in a display. Of course, if somebody doesn't like what we've put in, we'll change it. Up to now, though, that has never happened."

Fleurtations will also instal short-term floral displays for special events like open days and press conferences.

The challenge, though, remains in marketing the service. While every week, Belinda devotes a proportion of her time to tele-sales cold-calling, backed up by follow-up brochures, the bulk of new business is generated by word of mouth, and verbal endorsements from firms already on their books. In pitching for contracts, the most difficult aspect is getting customers to visualise what is on offer. Potential clients, while alive to the benefits of plant displays, generally have only the haziest notion of what they want. Very often, it is a case of the Managing Director shouting in passing to his secretary or someone in the personnel department: "Get some plants to brighten up the place."

Lack of knowledge on the part of the customer is the single greatest barrier to marketing that a company like Fleurtations faces. Unversed in plants or how they can best be deployed to good decorative effect, the client company seldom is in a position to make an informed choice between rival tenders. At best, from catalogue photographs showing different types of displays, buyers will indicate a rough price range which is acceptable. But on actual content, there are never any detailed company specifications issued on which to base tenders. The interior landscaping firms, themselves, are left to decide what should be included in the tender. Thus companies competing for the business rarely find they are operating from the same yardstick

When the rival quotations come in, buyers still don't really know what they are looking at, or how to differentiate between them. On paper, all bids look remarkably similar. The densities of plants and foliage so crucial to the look of a good display, in cold print, are not readily apparent. Confronted with unfamiliar plant names, and with little inkling of what the quantities really mean in physical appearance, the buyer quickly goes to the bottom line - and opts for the lowest tender. That the client is not judging like with like, and is attempting the fruitless task of trying to compare apples with oranges, makes no matter. Pitching for a contract therefore can be a somewhat frustrating business.

Establishing clear blue water between themselves and a competitor is extremely difficult. Belinda puts it this way: "We are all selling roughly the same range of plants. We can all say we offer a super maintenance service, and the company has no way of knowing if that is really the case. It has nothing to compare it with... I know for a fact that we give a much better density of plants in our displays than some other companies; I also genuinely believe we offer a top of the range maintenance service which is better than most. But getting that message over is hard. There is no easy way to explain the differences. In the end, it nearly always comes down to price, because that is the only yardstick companies are familiar with."

In fiercely competitive tendering, to land some important contracts, Fleurtations has had to supply plants and pots virtually at cost, knowing that it will eventually make its profit from the maintenance service supplied.

Belinda realises, though, that for Fleurtations truly to come out well ahead of the pack, her marketing techniques are going to have to break new ground, and she is currently casting around for the right way of getting her company message across in a way which is highly distinctive. That is no easy task. But it will have to be achieved if she is to attain her goal of eventually having a staff of 40 servicing Scotland. Backed by Belinda's bubbly personality, enthusiasm and business drive, that ambition does not seem to be an impossible dream.

CHAPTER SEVEN

Free-wheeling to success

IN today's world of hi-tech communication, simple business ideas which barely touch upon new technology can also achieve success. Courier services are a good example. They are a vital cog in the smooth running of commerce. Without them, huge tracts of business would find themselves missing important deadlines. Graphics and production houses would have difficulty in getting artwork to clients or printing houses on time; law firms would have to find new methods of getting contracts and legal documents physically delivered to other lawyers to clinch deals for clients. Across the whole spectrum of business, companies would find themselves in severe disarray. Courier services are a bit like elephant guns on a safari. In the course of a day you may not need to use them often; but when you do require them, you need them rather badly. Yet the format messenger services employ has scarcely changed from the days of the First World War motor cycle dispatch rider ferrying Army Generals' orders to officers at the front line.

When Adam Syme, now 29, decided to set up his own business messenger service, City Centre Couriers, in Edinburgh he took it one step further - or rather, backwards. His couriers rely, not on motor cycles, but on pedal power to deliver packages and letters around the Capital. Both for environmental reasons and efficiency, he only employs cyclists for city centre work. Today he has around 170 clients on his books.

That he has correctly judged his market is not in doubt. In a client survey he recently carried out, of those businesses which responded, all said they were happy with the service; 93 per cent considered his delivery times good; 99 per cent believed his prices were competitive (in fact, some said they were too low); 89 per cent indicated they used his service because it was environmentally sound; and 88 per cent stated they would be interested in using the ecologically friendly gas-fuelled van he has recently added to his fleet to service businesses in Edinburgh's hinterland. At his HQ in Marchmont Road, Edinburgh, Adam Syme is a happy man. Those are the sort of client responses most company Managing Directors would kill for.

With low capital outlays and self-employed staff, courier services are relatively cheap to set up. Finding a new approach in what is a fiercely competitive market is not easy. In Adam's case, his "back to the future" idea was nearly seven years in the making as he went off to do other things in his professional life.

The son of an art teacher, Adam left James Gillespie High School at the age of 16 with a single Higher Art pass and a clutch of Ordinary Level passes, and a fairly generalised idea that he would like to go to Art School. A further joust with the educational system, in the form of Further Education courses to try and upgrade some of his O-Levels, convinced him that the life of a student was not for him. At the time, he was working part-time as a sales assistant in an art shop in Edinburgh New Town. It was a job he thoroughly enjoyed. Selling materials taught him a great deal about their applications and many of the practicalities of the art world. Imbued, though, with a certain restlessness, he decided to move on.

Aged 17, he spotted in his local Job Centre a post with a well-known city law firm as a company messenger. He went to work for them, shuttling documents around Edinburgh's legal fraternity on a motor cycle provided by the firm. Stuck in many a traffic jam in the city centre, Adam reflected how much easier it would be to get around by bicycle. It was perhaps a fairly natural thought for the teenager. Although a motor cycle enthusiast himself - he then owned two Japanese classic machines, triple two-stroke Kewasiki 400s which he had acquired for about £200 each - his first, and lasting, love was cycling. A member of a cycle club, he regularly competed in road races and loved being out in the open air. Threading his way along Princes Street, he reckoned ordinary cycles would cope much better with traffic conditions. It was a thought which was to lie dormant for the next seven years.

Adam's next career move, in 1985, was in an entirely different direction. He became a cartographic draftsman for the Nature Conservancy Council (now

Scottish Natural Heritage). The post engaged both Adam's artistic talents and love of outdoor activity. Covering the Council's South East Region, which extended across an area stretching from Berwick to Perthshire and almost to Stirling, he seemed to have found the perfect job. It regularly took him out into the open countryside on surveying expeditions. In the office, he enjoyed the creativity of producing maps and graphic signs for erection in areas of special interest. He also took on board the Council's photographic requirements and spent many enjoyable hours in the darkroom processing his work. Some of the tasks, though, were exacting. As a draftsman he had to hand-produce duplicates of many of the maps he created, it being a period when computer graphics were still not in general use. "It was quite painstaking and a bit of a slog because quite a lot of duplicates were required. It was very fine work," he recalls.

Adam remained in the job for five years. "In the end, though, I decided to leave," he said. "It was getting too restrictive. I wasn't getting out of the office as much, and although I worked hard, and the job was quite well paid, I think I always knew that some day I'd be working for myself."

A flurry of jobs followed. Over the next few months, Adam worked as a cycle shop mechanic, a sound engineer setting up PA systems for conferences, a flower delivery man and a British Airport Authority baggage handler. The multiple roles were by choice. After five years of working for one organisation, Adam wanted variety. He didn't want to get into a rut. In his spare time, though, he had already begun developing his idea to start a courier service. Chatting with a friend in a pub one night, he also learned of an organisation, IMS Training and Development, which could help him further his ambition. Attending its courses in Edinburgh for nearly four months, he learned about the basics of starting up a business, from researching his potential client base and the competition to the more mundane, but equally vital, disciplines of taxation, book-keeping, cash flow auditing and preparation of a business plan.

"When I was starting up there were probably about eight to ten courier firms around, but I reckoned there was still room for me," says Adam. "Edinburgh is a small, compact city. At that time - although it is beginning to change now - the bulk of the business community was situated very much within a very small area and I was sure bikes were the answer."

Before sending out a questionnaire to 100 firms, Adam had first to define his business, and decide its true identity. That was a most important exercise because from it flowed the core marketing strategy he has followed right up to the present day. In his evaluation, Adam decided that what made him different from everyone else in his sector was the fact that he was going to offer a service which, above everything else, was environmentally friendly and didn't add to city pollution levels. That factor - and not price (which lay in the middle range of rates charged by courier services) - became his principal selling tool. The big question was: Did companies want it? While the environmental movement had gained the general public's support, would commercial interests regard Adam's entry into the courier market as anything other than a praiseworthy, if limited fringe delivery service?

Large companies are the world's supreme pragmatists, and there was one blindingly obvious conclusion to be drawn from a courier business completely reliant on bicycles as transport: In terms of the distances it could cover, it was severely limited. It was only going to provide an extremely localised service. More-over, pedal cyclists could only handle non-bulky material to a maximum weight of 5 kilos (approximately 11 lbs). Was that sufficient to meet their needs? To find out, Adam set about hand-delivering his questionnaires to city centre companies. He also personally collected them in, to ensure he got a full return of responses. Firms which expressed strong interest in the service were then targeted for follow-up approaches with brochures. From that exercise, he netted three clients who said they would use his service. "One was a solicitors, the second was a type-setting firm and I forget now what the third one was," says Adam.

City Centre Couriers, at its inception, was strictly a one-man operation. Its HQ was the front room of Adam's ground-floor flat in Marchmont Road (it still is). His equipment consisted of a brand new mountain bike purchased for £315; a mobile phone which, because of a "dead" area around his flat, couldn't pick up messages; and a large black and yellow PVC delivery bag. Well, not quite. In expectation of expansion, and to get a good trade price, the young entrepreneur had confidently bought six delivery bags for a fleet of couriers who were as yet no more than a business twinkle in his eye.

In January, 1991, City Centre Couriers began trading. On his first day, in his smart new livery of black and yellow, Adam hung around pre-selected spots in the city centre, waiting for the mobile phone to ring. It was cold and there was snow on the ground. His mobile rang just once that first day - a delivery which earned him the less than princely sum of £1 70. But he was on his way.

To finance the fledgling company, Adam was in receipt of £40 a week under the Enterprise Allowance Scheme. He also had put up £1500 of his own money and had obtained a £1500 low interest loan from the Prince's Scottish Youth Business Trust. He had obtained a small amount of sponsorship from an environmental organisation, LEAP (Lothian and Edinburgh Environmental

Partnership) which financed the production of his initial brochures. In his first year of operations, he also ploughed in a £250 prize which he won in a Scottish Enterprise Livewire business competition. There was also available a bank overdraft facility of £500.

Within a month, Adam took on his first courier to help handle the increasing volume of business. By March he had built up a client list of 12 companies and was ready to take the next step forward, getting a licence to instal a two-way radio-control system which would do away with the costly and cumbersome necessity of being reliant upon mobile phones for communication. The first system he bought cost, in total, almost £3000. It was a considerable expense for a small company to take on, but it proved its financial worth in just seven days. Within a week, his client list more than doubled from 12 to a total of 30. "I had a lot of clients waiting to come to me when I became radio-controlled," said Adam. "So as soon as I informed them, I got their business. There was a really big jump in the workload."

Today the company has four full-time couriers working for it, with Adam acting as dispatcher, handling an average of 100 calls a day. The radio console these days has been upgraded to a VHF system, which is much more suitable for outdoor work than the old controls, which have found a new lease of life at the ground of Hibernian F.C. as an internal communications system.

There can be little doubt that the "green" image Adam has fostered for his business has been a key component in its growth. In the beginning, as he readily admits, it cost him a lot of potential business from firms looking for a more conventional motorised service which could deliver to a much wider catchment area. However, there is a plus side. Environment-conscious clients remain loyal to the service; his cycle couriers, too, are a lot less forbidding looking than the anonymous, helmet-clad messengers who lumber into many offices. Adam says, "Motor cycle couriers can be a pretty gruff lot. That's probably because their stress levels are a lot higher than our cyclists. Exercise gets rid of stress and tension, and cycling, while it can be tiring, is an enjoyable thing to do. I never have any problem in getting cycle couriers. In fact, I've a backlog of people wanting the job. They range in age from 16 to their early forties."

Since commencing trading, Adam has seen company turn-over rise steadily. In its first year the business made just £10,000. Now in its sixth year, it is heading for £100,000, with the prospect of major increases to come by the end of the year.

The big leap forward will be occasioned by the arrival of Adam's first vehicle to extend his delivery range. Until now, City Centre Couriers has been able to cover, by bicycle, deliveries throughout the city centre and as far out as the city's airport. But the complexion of Edinburgh's business life is changing. There has been considerable growth of companies on the outskirts of the city, where rates are less punitive. Responsive to that change, Adam decided to take on motorised transport. To maintain his company's"green" credentials, he scoured the country for a suitable option. Eventually he came up with a Ford Escort van which he had specially customised by a firm in Milton Keynes to run on natural gas. Putting it on the road cost the company a total of £12,700.

The addition of the van, he knows, is set to change quite dramatically the complexion of the company. The high level of interest expressed by clients on its arrival, in response to Adam's survey, indicates that they will want it to make deliveries for them at least across the Central Belt. "I'm probably going to have to add a second vehicle pretty quickly," says Adam. "You can't raise people's expectations and then disappoint them. I'm already looking at the possibility of buying an electric-powered vehicle. My original plans were simply to use the gas-fuelled van to cover the outskirts of the city and out as far as South Queensferry and Dalkeith, but that may not prove possible if customers are looking for deliveries to Glasgow and other towns. If that happens, I'm going to require a second vehicle."

With possibly two vehicles on the road, City Centre Couriers will be offering clients a much more complete service. Until now, of necessity, many customers have employed a two-tier approach to meet their business needs, employing City Centre Couriers cyclists for localised work and another conventional motorised company for deliveries further afield. For the first time, Adam can combine both those options in a single, "all round" service. Creeping into the business equation, though, is something of an ethical decision for the young entrepreneur: How "green" is "green?" His company already enjoys the official imprimatur of LEAF. Every time it sends out information to companies inquiring about the possibility of using, say, recycled paper in their operations, the organisation includes a City Centre Couriers brochure - on the logical grounds that if a firm is keen to find out about environmentally friendly business methods, it may be interested also in employing an environmentally conscious messenger service. If that service were to become "top heavy" and dominated by the use of motorised transport - albeit powered by "clean" fuel methods - the company image changes fairly radically.

To some that may seem an overly purist viewpoint of the environmentalist movement. Nevertheless it remains a very real consideration. A company which exists by virtue of being ecology-conscious is judged by a different set of standards than normal commerce. Its very selling strengths are also its limitations.

It is perhaps for that reason Adam is adamant that motorised transport will never supplant his fleet of cyclist couriers. Eventually he envisages that the business will require about 20 cycle messengers if it continues to expand at its present rate. "There will always be a need for them in the city," he says. "Until now they have all been self-employed but this year I plan on taking them onto a PAYE system as staff. It's going to cost more, but that's the way I'd like the company to go."

There is a lot of common sense and shrewdness in that approach. In a society which indisputably is seriously deficient in harbouring its natural resources, a company which gainfully employs a substantial number of people through a healthful, non-contentious activity like cycling is more likely to engage the affections of the "green" public. If to grow and prosper it has to broaden its business methods to include forms of motorised transport, the pill has been sweetened. In this world, nothing is perfect.

That said, it should be noted that in 1993 Adam Syme's tiny company, in competition against many household names within Scottish business, received a commendation for its contribution to the environment. At the outset he was willing to eschew fast profits in favour of preserving the company ethos; he may well find he will have to do so again. It is something of a tightrope act. For certain, on the congested, fume-laden streets of Edinburgh - the penance we pay to live in all cities - his cyclist couriers are a most welcome addition.

AT the other end of the spectrum in the courier service industry is Bullet Express, a vigorously growing young Glasgow-based company which is heading confidently towards its first £1 million turn-over after a little more than five years' trading. Run by two cousins, David McCutcheon, 33, and Gary Smith, 31, it today offers an impressive range of services across the UK, Northern Ireland, Eire and also into Western Europe.

With a workforce of about 24, including a dozen self-employed contract drivers, it has at its disposal a fleet of some 19 vehicles ranging from small courier vans to a 17.5 tonne container lorry, and has just staffed up a new office in Edinburgh, based at the city's airport.

Very much in the "from an elephant to a thimble" business, among the odder items Bullet Express has delivered have been Cracker TV scripts to star Robbie Coltrane at his Scottish home; world champion Stephen Hendry's personal snooker queue which was urgently needed for a tournament; big match away strips for Celtic F.C.; and even a former Rangers player's favourite boots which he had forgotten to take with him when he transferred to Everton.

Its core business, however, lies in less exotic items: The fast, reliable delivery of company goods. By the pallet-load or the lorry-load, all is grist to the mill. From straight-forward merchandise to delicate electronic equipment; from automotive spare parts to engineering equipment, Bullet Express offers a same-day delivery service throughout the United Kingdom, 24 hours a day, 365 days a year, plus a wide variety of additional services, including next day and 9am delivery across Britain.

"In this business," says David, "you are only as good as your next delivery. Reliability and meeting deadlines are everything because very often it's a distress delivery. It could be a spare part urgently needed to get machinery operational again or an important tender document on a contract worth hundreds of thousands of pounds which has to be on someone's desk for a closing deadline. Nothing we deliver is ever left hanging around in an office or a warehouse. If the consignment isn't on the doorstep within five minutes of when you said it would be, someone from that company is on the phone asking where it is."

In the delivery industry, customer satisfaction is all-important. It is even more crucial than price. David says, "Many firms aren't looking for the cheapest service. They are looking for reliability. Our prices are pretty competitive, but the real reason we retain customer loyalty is because of our high standards of service."

These days, as a slick, highly professional organisation, Bullet Express enjoys the respect of its peers in what is an extremely competitive market place. However, the road to success was not one automatically paved with gold. The company's formative years, to say the least, were ruggedly character-forming. Just about every aspect of the company's struggle for survival in those early years proved a baptism of fire. But then what can one expect of a company whose name, Bullet Express, was a tongue in cheek reference, not as might be supposed, to the speed of its operations, but to the number of times its joint founder David McCutcheon had found himself on the wrong end of a P45 pay-off slip?

The Chinese, who give considerable thought to naming businesses, and who choose only the most propitious symbols for good luck, may well have a point. A more mixed beginning to the life of a new company would be difficult to envisage. The coming together of the two cousins followed no less intriguing separate career patterns which might best be described as being of the "lucky white heather" variety.

Gary Smith, who like his cousin, was educated at Cathkin High School, left at 16 to train under his tradesman father as a joiner. In business, father and son relationships - particularly ones where direct parental supervision is involved - can be fairly highly charged arenas and so it proved for Gary. It was not a success. Within a few months, he decided joinering was not for him and cast around for a new trade. It was the early eighties, a time when the massive housing refurbishment, which had been going on full tilt across the city was edging into recession, but he was successful in gaining a job as an apprentice electrician. That fledgling career came to an abrupt end. While working on the roof of a property in Helenvale Street, Parkhead, Gary spotted Celtic football star Bobby Lennox out training young club players in a nearby park. To get a better view he clambered over the roof ridge to the other side, and lost his footing on tiles which, unknown to him, were covered in ice. He plummeted 30ft into the street below, breaking his nose and four front teeth.

When he recovered, he became a panel beater and spray painter with his uncle. A few years later there was a brief, and unsuccessful, foray into the Merchant Navy as a cook. He quit after just three months, because he kept getting seasick. Back on dry land, Gary would have liked to resume training as an electrician, but couldn't find an opening so he returned to panel beating and paint spraying in his uncle's business - although he always knew it was not going to be his final occupation.

Meanwhile his cousin David had been experiencing a similarly chequered career. From school, which he left early, he joined a steel fabrication company in Glasgow as a manual worker in the yard. It wasn't long before he caught the eye of a member of the sales team, who recognised his potential, and arranged for him to be moved onto the sales staff. Surviving the tough, no nonsense sales training, culled very much from the school of hard knocks, David began to show considerable aptitude for the work and later moved on as a salesman to a steel stockholding company in South Street, Glasgow. However, it closed down and he was made redundant.

A good salesman, it wasn't long before David bounced back - this time into furniture retail, first as a customer sales manager with MFI, then about a year later with Reid Furniture as a customer services manager. When the company retrenched and started laying off staff, one of that number was David. Nothing daunted, he moved on, this time into the freighting and transport world. He joined Orion Freight. It was a period of acute recession when Scottish firms were going down like ninepins, and David's run of misfortune continued. Just six months after he joined the company, it went into liquidation.

At about this stage, most people might have been forgiven for becoming a little paranoid about employment prospects, but the ever resilient David moved on, this time to become a salesman with the freight company, Parcel Line, based in Bellshill, Lanarkshire. Once again he excelled at his job, but even here all was not plain sailing; David found himself regularly at loggerheads with management over changes to its sales bonus targets. Somewhat naively, he objected to the way that new sales goals were imposed every time sales staff hit their targets. He complained that the company was moving the goal posts. That friction was to culminate in a bizarre episode when, in one and the same day, he was awarded a bottle of champagne by the company for being salesman of the month and was then sacked and divested of his company car. One of the sales reps had to give him a lift home in his old company car.

For some months David had been eagerly awaiting a new replacement vehicle. As the pair drove off, David winced as the gleaming new rep's car, which he had hand-picked, pulled in. Finally deposited on his own doorstep, a disconsolate David watched his old car - and his career - disappear round the corner, then realised belatedly that his house keys were still lying in its glove department. The keys were brought back to him a couple of hours later. Their delivery, however, did not signal the end of his travails on that particularly bleak day. That night, while he was out, raiders burgled his home.

Bowing to the inevitability of the fates, David decided to work for himself.

Despite his differences with Parcel Line, David had gained a lot of knowledge about the freight courier industry. In particular, he believed that same-day delivery - a service which Parcel Line had instituted, then pulled out of - was a field which offered a newcomer a bright future. As sales manager for the ceased service, he had plenty of contacts among companies which had used it with his former company. Now working for himself, he contacted a number of them, offering to set up the service once more.

He had one personal proviso: It would have to operate to high professional standards. In his time with Parcel Line he had not been overly impressed with the small-time operators he had encountered elsewhere. Many were unreliable. Having contracted for haulage runs, some would fail to turn up or would arrive many hours late. Others didn't use professional drivers, but relied on untrained casual drivers to find their way round Britain. David had no intention of embarking upon a slap-dash operation. From his initial trawl round the companies he secured one contract - so with a partner, and working from home, he started up Bullet Express.

It was during that first year that Gary joined the company as its first employee. Anxious to escape the drudgery of panel beating, at David's request, he moved to the fledgling company, which by now had just moved into a small unit in Dalmarnock Road. His weekly pay packet was lighter, but Gary reckoned the temporary sacrifice was worth it. Here was an opportunity for him to get in on the ground floor and grow with the company. There was another reason, too. He and his cousin had always been great friends, and there was a strong bond of trust between them.

The first crucial 12 months of trading for any company tend to be rather fraught. There are steep learning curves to be gone through, coupled with tight finance and a huge investment of energy in gaining customers. Bullet Express was no exception. But it coped.

Very soon afterwards, though, it underwent a radical change when the partnership was dissolved. Originally, David planned to sell out his share of the business to his partner, then start up his own company along with Gary. He even had a name picked out for the new company, UK Sameday. But fairly late in the proceedings, by mutual consent, the deal was reversed: David bought out his partner. Legal documents were drawn up and the original partnership was dissolved, with David and Gary taking over the business. "It was brilliant. It suited everyone all round," said David.

The euphoria of the moment in getting a fresh start, was somewhat tempered by one of the company's three precious second hand vans being written off - on the very day the change of ownership was legally sealed.

In the months that followed, with two second hand vans, the new joint owners worked at a frantic pace, delivering orders up and down the country. In the busier weeks it became a standing joke that about the only time they saw each other was when they waved to each other as their vans passed around Kendal - one heading back to Scotland and the other going on an outward run. It was a difficult year's trading, one of the principal drawbacks being the lack of time they had to seek out new business. Most of their time was spent on the road. Whenever they could, however, they spent a few days going out leafleting companies about their services - then would have to stop because of the volume of extra work it generated. By dint of the pair working round the clock, at the end of their first year in partnership the company had grossed a turn-over of £90,000, a very creditable achievement.

There was not much time, however, for the two young businessmen to linger over that success. In their second year, they learned the hard way about the risks of having too many eggs in one basket. Their single biggest customer drastically reduced the rates it paid for Bullet Express's courier services.

It came about when David took out a franchise with the England-based company in a bid to safeguard several lucrative Scottish areas Bullet Express was covering for it. The runs appeared to be under threat. But the deal quickly turned sour. Under the franchise, Bullet Express found its rates were virtually halved and it was also confronted by a fairly substantial list of hidden extra costs. What had been entered into as a protective measure ended in litigation.

Fortunately for Bullet Express, it had wasted only a month going down what turned out to be a blind alley. The hard truth is that franchisee courier companies by and large are expected to make their money on the return legs of their journeys - filling their empty vehicles for the homeward trip. Scotland is a nett exporter of freight; it doesn't have the same rich volume of two-way traffic in goods which exists all over England.

The sudden and unexpected reversal, though, forced David and Gary into major company economies. By now the business was supporting a total of five. That had to be cut back to just the two principals. They also gave up the office, saving themselves around £200 a week, and returned to working from David's bedroom. Despite the severity of the cutbacks the cousins never lost their faith in the business. Optimistically, they asked British Telecom to hold for them their special phone number, 647 - 6000.

"We always knew we would be back," says Gary. "At the time, giving up the office wasn't a major problem. We were hardly in the place, anyway. Most of the time we were out on the road."

For the young entrepreneurs the biggest problem of being without premises for a six-month spell was not having a place to prepare goods for delivery. "Many's the time we were out in the car park, in the back of the van, labelling parcels until two in the morning in the dark. The hours we put in were horrendous," recalls David.

Like all sharp, and salutary lessons - if your company survives them - the setback in the long run was to work to Bullet Express's advantage. It forced David to become much more selective in his customer base. He began to target major blue chip companies within the transport industry, focusing, initially, on next day 9 am deliveries, which those organisations weren't equipped to handle. While the returns were not as high as same day delivery, Bullet Express was virtually guaranteed daily work - and, just as important, fast, regular payment. The company's cash flow quickly improved. By the end of 1992, the company had moved back into its old office and was back in the black. It had also managed to take on two more drivers - answering one of its most pressing needs, which was to free David and Gary on alternate weeks from driving to handle administration and sales. "It didn't make sense for us both to be on the road when one of us, working from the office, could be pulling in more business," says Gary. "It wasn't a correct use of our resources."

For Bullet Express, the years of real growth were 1993 and 1994. By bringing in sub-contractor drivers in 1993, David was freed to do what he did best ... selling his company's services to companies. As the firm grew, so too did the duo's confidence. They invested in company uniforms to give Bullet Express a smart, corporate image and - well ahead of their time - installed a £3,500, ultra-modern radio system which allowed them to keep in constant touch with drivers where-ever they were in the UK.

They also relocated into bigger and better offices in Glasgow Road, with a good-sized yard. But still the fates weren't finished with them. David recalls, "We'd done a really good deal and had the use of a good, big yard. We really felt we were getting places. Without a word of a lie, we had only been in the office literally one day when the guy who'd leased it to us walked in and told us his company was going into liquidation."

Thinking it through, after the initial shock had worn off, the cousins decided to sit tight. They reckoned the Receiver would still be interested in making money from the property while the former owner's business was being wound up. And so it transpired. When the property was taken over later by Fridge Freight, Bullet Express leased their offices from the new owners. David said, "It was a very good arrangement. We got on extremely well with the new owners and even picked up a bit of work from them."

By August of 1993, they were able to put two brand new vans on the road. "We sat down and looked at all our repair bills for vehicles and discovered it was actually going to be cheaper to invest in new vans," said David, "so that is what we did."

For the first time, too, that year the pair acquired company cars. It came about in rather odd fashion. On a day when the cousins had just put four extra vans on the road, they walked out into the yard animatedly talking about their plans for the business - to discover they had no transport. All the vehicles were out. "Everybody was away home in new vans and we had nothing," said David. "We looked at each other and said, 'This is ridiculous.' "

For the next few months the company continued to grow, solidly if unspectacularly. Then came a long overdue lucky break which transformed the fortunes of Bullet Express. One Friday, David received a phone call from a business contact in a major company, saying: "Come and see me."

At the meeting, he learned that a large courier firm, Shuttle Direct, which transported their goods, was about to cease trading that evening. David's friend told him: "We want you to take over deliveries for us on Monday."

It was the breakthrough Bullet Express needed. Overnight, its annual turnover was set to double. That one contract, alone, was worth £100,000. Bullet Express was also in excellent shape to exploit the fairly large gap in the market left by the demise of Shuttle Direct. Immediately Bullet Express launched a month-long advertising campaign on Radio Clyde, hoping to pick up more new business, and netted a number of other important contracts. By the end of 1994, turn-over had leaped from £110,000 to £240,000 and Bullet Express had built up a substantial fleet of 19 vehicles.

One other result of Bullet Express's rapid expansion was that it had to sharpen up its financial act, and pay a lot more attention to its billing procedures. With the help of its bank, it instituted new finance and credit control structures to pull in more quickly the money it was owed. "In a business with a turn-over of £100,000 lying out £5000 wasn't too serious. But when suddenly our turn-over had more than doubled and amounts due were running to £20,000 to £30,000 it was a different matter. If somebody went down, owing us a lot of money, it could have affected us pretty badly," said David. "Common sense dictated we had to sort it out. No matter how big the customer is, you shouldn't be afraid to ask for your money."

Practising what he preached, David actually arranged with some of his biggest customers new payments schedules to ensure Bullet Express's cash flow was on a much sounder footing.

The following year an appearance on Scottish Television's Business Game, sponsored by Scottish Enterprise and Bank of Scotland, further boosted the company's fortunes. The TV appearance raised general awareness of the company within business circles. With that higher public profile came additional contracts. To handle the increased volume of trade, Bullet Express brought in an experienced full-time transport manager to handle its operations.

In business, momentum is everything. Having survived all that life could throw at them, Gary and David could now be said to be on a roll. Having first personally checked out the runs, the company began venturing into Europe. It now does regular trips to France, Germany and Italy for customers. Via Europhones, it keeps in constant touch with its two-man driving teams while they are on the road.

The most recent company development has been the introduction of a completely new service, a guaranteed next day delivery to Northern Ireland, five days a week, plus a two-day guaranteed delivery to Eire, through a hook-up with an Irish freighting company.

David says, "We meet our partner at Stranraer every night, who takes the goods over by ferry. All consignments are in Belfast by 3am, which gives them time to service the surrounding areas for 9am. The Irish service is being built up steadily. Our partners handle delivery of goods for us in Ireland and we do the same for them on this side."

While nowadays it has good storage facilities at its HQ in Millcroft Road, on Shawfield Industrial Estate, the company's rapid expansion is likely to mean another move to larger premises. "We are actively looking for a new office," says David.

A bright and vigorous future for Bullet Express looks in prospect. That is no more than the cousins' due. A tougher baptism in business would be hard to find. As David says, it sounds a bit of a horror story, when the various incidents are strung together. "Fortunately, they didn't happen all at once. You just worked your way through the problem and got on with things until the next one arose," he added.

He makes it sound simpler than the reality. The reversals of fortune would have floored many lesser spirits. Instead of becoming embittered or alienated, they picked themselves up, dusted themselves down and got on with the business of living. If ever they decide to rename the company (after suitable consultation with a Chinese astrologer, of course) a suitable one would be, True Grit.

CHAPTER EIGHT

Different styles of fashion business

IN THE world of fashion, as we watch the carefully choreographed drama of the catwalk, and the models who gracefully glide across our vision in stunningly elegant confections, the commodity on sale is not clothes. It is dreams.

That is as true for the international salons of the world-famous fashion houses whose designers by some mysterious process (to which lesser mortals are not privy) decree what the new season's look is to be as it is in the slightly less high-voltage world of smaller design houses which sell their own exclusive lines to the merely affluent, as opposed to the seriously rich.

For both, the sales talk with clients may revolve around colours, daring combinations of fabrics and accessories, hem line lengths, cuts, drapes, folds, pleats, darts, intricate stitching, exclusive types of buttons and buttonholes, but these are but the common clay of the potter. The technical expertise of such establishments in transforming the raw material we may also take for granted; they would not be operating at this end of the fashion spectrum if they had not in their employ staff skilled in the art of dress-making. The reality is that, one and all, they are selling romance, allure and a feeling of being special. It does not matter, either, whether the purchaser is seeking a limited edition, off the peg haute couture design or a made to measure garment.

When a woman crosses the threshold of an expensive retail outlet of a fashion house she enters a fantasy world where she is cosseted from head to toe. Around her flutter knowledgeable, deferential assistants, proffering, when asked, advice on different materials and styles and coming up with suggestions on how the clients' own ideas on dress style can be successfully incorporated. No detail is too small or too inconsequential to be mulled over at length. Alternative solutions are fulsomely considered and finally ruled upon; remember, this is an industry where success or failure may hinge on something as small as the placing of a buttonhole. Outside of the actual fittings, it is not uncommon for assistants to spend more than an hour with individual clients, guiding them through the great adventure of selecting a special outfit costing £300 to £500 or a wedding dress where there will be precious little change out of £1500.

Throughout the whole process, in both the initial visit or during subsequent fittings, the Rolls Royce personalised service purrs smoothly onwards, merchandising dreams to clothe often too, too prosaically solid flesh. This is fantasy land but one remove from the pages of a romantic novel, with the client cast as the heroine. It is also hard work.

Romantic heroines, in real life, can be hard taskmistresses. They demand, and get, last-minute changes, putting already tight deadlines under enormous pressure. If perfection does not come cheaply, neither does the cost, to the couturier, of sustaining the illusion. Overheads are high. Running up the new range of styles for the season is but one of many heavy expenses. Premises in appearance have to be as opulent as lavish film sets. There are fashion shows and models to organise; expensive brochures and top quality studio photographic shoots to produce of new collections. Promoting the look and image of the design house is a never-ending cycle.

Behind the scenes, away from the glamour, a balance has to be kept on stock volumes of costly fabrics which may not be required for many months, and on staffing levels in what is a labour-intensive business. The world of the small, independent fashion house is a constant juggling of expensive, showbiz-style promotional glitz and hard-nosed economics, and it is extremely easy in the high pressure excitement of it all to get the numbers wrong. Like the world of fashion, itself, success may be something of an illusion. All is not always what it seems. In an industry where publicity is its life's blood, there is not a design house in the country, which, on some occasion, hasn't found itself being lauded to the skies for fulfilling a prestigious contract with great style and panache - only for it to discover, when the final returns are in, that after all its hard work it has merely broken even, or worse, made a small loss.

The reasons for this may vary. The special contract may have so disrupted normal production that it has lost out on regular, "bread and butter" work. Or the design house may have encountered a number of unexpected "add on" production costs, such as slow delivery of quantities of fabrics, which disrupt normal cost-effective production methods, and require the company to hire in unbudgeted for additional help to meet deadlines. Whatever the individual reasons, such poor return ventures may usually be ascribed to one general, fundamental cause: To take on the contract, the company has stepped beyond the boundaries of its normal resources and working practices. The pressures being what they are, the life of an independent design house can often be like that of the dragonfly: Iridescently beautiful but short-lived.

The sad truth, also, is that Scotland, for all its many talented designers, is not on the main international fashion circuit. Somewhere in the region of 70 to 80 per cent of our designers end up moving to London, Europe or the USA in search of opportunities to express their creativity and flair.

With the advent of the Garden Festival in the 1980s, it looked as if Glasgow was about to establish a toehold on international fashion. From the festival blossomed a city's renewed belief in itself. It fairly crackled with creative energy; there was a buzz and an excitement about Glasgow which captivated all who came in contact with it. The world discovered Glasgow Style. Writers for international magazines descended upon the city, to record for readers its vigorous arts scene and its young designers. That design spotlight remained upon the city right up to, and throughout, City of Culture Year. But when the music stopped, and the last fireworks flared, the world's fashion buyers were still settling into chairs in executive hotel suites in London, New York and Milan. "It was as if a huge plug was pulled on New Year's Eve, and we were told, 'You've had your year. That's it for the rest of the decade,'" observed one Glasgow designer.

In reality, Glasgow had had a long run, fairly centre stage, on the international catwalk, and had established - or, more accurately, re-established - its credentials as a city bristling with design talent. But, like Barcelona, another city steeped in innovative design and dramatic flair, it was finding that talent, alone, is not enough. Geographic location is important, too. It is easier to relocate new designers than create on the rim of Europe new international fashion centres, with all the attendant infra-structures required.

This is not an indictment of Scotland's lively fashion scene, or of the international reputation it enjoys in both traditional knitwear and innovative fashion design. But the realities of life are such that the big challenge for independent design houses in Scotland is to find and develop a market which allows them to live, work and remain in their own country.

The Next Generation

Two companies which have done so with considerable success are By Storm, from Bearsden, and Lex McFadyen Design, which might be described as a veteran of the eighties Glasgow design scene. Although today operating much in the same market place, they do so in markedly different manner. By Storm is setting off on a trail which its founder, designer Joyce Young, hopes will see it operate within an international market from a Scottish base. Lex McFadyen's goals are a little more relaxed, and firmly embedded in the lifestyle he wishes to create for himself. The aim is to create for himself the space to concentrate on design, rather than embark upon major business expansion, although he will embrace it should suitable opportunities present themselves. His company might be said to have developed organically, rather than along strictly laid down business goals.

Hearteningly for young designers, both methods have proved equally viable.

Joyce Young's route to designing for the catwalk might be said almost to have been pre-ordained. The youngest in a family of three (she has two brothers 14 years and eight years older than herself), Joyce's interest in fashion was present from an early age. At her home in Saltcoats, Ayrshire, from the age of seven she used to sketch out, then make all her dolls' clothes, running them up on her mother's sewing machine at the kitchen table. At the age of 10 she had graduated to making her own clothes. It was accepted by her parents - her father was an accounts clerk and her mother a teacher - that Joyce was a highly creative young girl, and at Ardrossan Academy, her artistic bent shone through strongly. At the age of 17, on completion of her Higher-level exams, she enrolled at Glasgow School of Art on a four-year course, studying interior design, embroidery and weaving. At that time, the Art School had no courses in fashion, but Joyce, an enthusiastic and hard-working student, soon found herself roped into helping stage the school's fashion shows, all of which added to her experience. "I just loved working with fabrics and colours," she says.

After completing her degree in 1975 she very quickly obtained a job with a Glasgow company, S. & P. Harris, later taken over by Bairdwear, which mass manufactured clothes for Marks & Spencer. It was a time when the retail giant was asking its satellite manufacturers to set up their own design departments to produce for it a regular flow of new designs and concepts. Impressed at the interview by Joyce's voluminous portfolio, the Bairdwear management hired her for the new post. Joyce's brief was to set up the manufacturers' internal design department.

For a young girl of 21, straight out of art school and with no hands-on experience of the rag trade, it was a very considerable responsibility. But the company, too, was feeling its way. This was a new development in its trading with Marks & Spencer, and it wasn't about to commit itself overly heavily until it saw how the system was going to bed in with its normal operations.

It was, to say the least, a formidable task. Creating a new department is always tough, but usually there is a degree of co-operation from other staff. Joyce had to do it completely on her own. Within the organisation, she says, there was heavy internal resistance to change and her role was viewed with suspicion, if not outright dislike. In the early days, not even the most basic of help was available to her. Her design department was a borrowed company seminar room where she worked sketching outfits. She had no assistant machinist to run up her samples, so she had to run up her own designs on her own machine, which she had brought into the office. Every week she would go to London with her portfolio of sketches to meet the Marks & Spencer selectors to discuss their requirements, then it was back to Glasgow to run up the amended designs and take down samples the following week. Frequently Joyce found herself working until 3am, finishing off designs and sketches, then she would be up again at 5am to prepare to catch the first flight down to London to present her concepts. Everything within her department she had to personally organise, right down to sorting out boxes of buttons.

On her London trips, for the first time, Joyce came face to face with the harsh financial realities of designing for the mass market. Everything was cost-driven. If a garment couldn't be produced for a specific price, it didn't get made. Time and again, the young designer would present sketches to the selectors, who would enthuse over their special features - then proceed to dispense with them one by one because they were too expensive. "They would love it, but then they would turn round to me and say. 'We need it at £12.99 so could you take the braids off and put on cheaper buttons,' " says Joyce. "It was very frustrating, but great experience."

After a year, frustrated by the commercial restrictions upon her work, Joyce decided to launch her own business. She went into partnership with another designer, Pamela Ross, and formed Sequin to produce up-market special occasion wear. The two young designers' work complemented each other, with Joyce having special skills in embroidery and Pamela in hand-painting fabrics. For two years their HQ was a spare room in Joyce's flat in Clouston Street in Glasgow's west end, taking their wares round Glasgow's up-market shops. They had begun by designing a lot of day wear, but after one of them, Daly's commissioned from them half a dozen wedding dresses, they were advised by the shop's buyer to switch to special occasion wear. "It was very good advice," says Joyce. "People are prepared to spend more on an outfit for a special occasion than they are on day wear."

As their name became better known, the two friends gained confidence. They took premises above the Rogano Restaurant in the city centre, took on a pattern cutter and two machinists and attempted to grow the business. By now, some shops were coming to them, seeking their new designs. Exhibiting at a trade design fair also widened their range of sales. They exported a range to Saudi Arabia, and also gained an entree to a London store, Dickins & Jones. But it was brutally hard work. The young designers were working virtually round the clock. Because everything was hand-produced, at night they would have to take home garments to try and complete them to keep the momentum going during the next day. Life was a constant round of train and car journeys, lugging around sample garments, then working flat-out at night to fulfil commitments. "We seemed to be working 24 hours a day, and the business had reached a plateau; we never managed to get the business beyond that stage," recalls Joyce. "One of the difficulties was that we hadn't the finance to make the next step. Whenever we went looking for small business grants, everyone told us we were doing so well we didn't need a grant. We felt we needed more finance to get to the next stage. We enjoyed what we were doing, but we weren't developing."

In 1981, Mother Nature took a hand. Both designers fell pregnant. They wound up Sequin, selling off the remainder of the lease and relocating their staff with a nearby shop. There were no debts, and the couple came out of the exercise with a small profit. Joyce, for a short period worked on her own on interior design. But it looked as if both she and Pamela were destined for lives of domesticity, with family needs taking precedence over career ambitions.

For fully five years Joyce who has two children, Susie, now aged 14, and Ian, 11, was absent from the fashion scene. But the creative hunger was still there. She entered a Britain-wide competition run by a washing machine company to design children's wear for Togs for Toddlers UK - and won. The prize was a washing machine and a holiday for four to the Caribbean. But more important to Joyce than the glamorous holiday, or the excitement of the press and TV coverage her success generated, was the realisation that she hadn't lost her touch as a designer.

Some weeks later, on a rather low day when she and her husband had just learned that they had been unsuccessful in a bid for a "perfect" new house, while idly leafing through a newspaper, Joyce spotted an advertisement for a post as Creative Designer for Marks & Spencer. Telling herself she was only doing so to keep her hand in at interview skills, Joyce applied for the post. "The next thing I knew I had a full-time job and was getting a nanny for the children," she says.

Again, her Marks & Spencer debut was marked by controversy. The Managing Director who had hired her, within weeks of her arrival, departed. No-one else quite knew what he had planned for her. She found herself attending meetings in London where no-one knew what she was supposed to be doing. "It was fairly chaotic, and a really strange atmosphere," she recalls.

However, the new management team eventually - and firmly - defined her role. As senior designer and design room manager, it was a hectic lifestyle. Every second day, Joyce would have to fly from Glasgow to London to attend top-level meetings. There were regular trips to international shows in Milan, New York and Paris. Her day often began at 5am and wasn't over until 9pm as she dashed for the last Shuttle from London Heathrow back to Scotland. However, this time round with Marks & Spencer she was approaching the job from a different perspective. Having run her own business, and experienced all its many challenges, she felt she had a great deal to offer over and beyond designing. Once again, though, when the gloss of being back at the centre of the rag trade had worn thin, she found herself becoming increasingly disenchanted with the bureaucracy and internal politics which, to her way of thinking, dominated the organisation. The constrictions upon creativity she also found increasingly irksome with the passage of the years. After six years with the company, matters came to a head. More and more, her regular trips from Glasgow to London had resulted in her having to stay overnight; now the company wanted her to move full-time to London. Joyce said No, and resigned. "It was an excellent opportunity for me to start my present business," she says. "All I needed to make the break was that little extra push."

Just one day after she left full-time employment, Joyce began a six-week business course run by Clydebank Local Enterprise Company, preparing a business plan for her new company, By Storm. On completing the course, her first port of call was the Clydesdale Bank to finance the restoration of a derelict cottage on Milngavie Road, Bearsden, which she wished to transform into the company's headquarters. It liked the business concept and was prepared to advance her £80,000.

Equally importantly, Joyce had also acquired a London partner who ran his own fashion business, a pleating and processing firm, Gale Force. The partnership was actually a great deal more important psychologically to Joyce than any financial benefit. What it gave her was access to another experienced business brain; someone who could assess the risks of expansion, then tell her: Go for it. Sequin had failed to develop its full potential because there was no-one around to give its two designers professional advice and encouragement.

On their own, Joyce and her then partner stayed small; they lacked the extra confidence needed to make the next strategic leap forward. With a partner involved in By Storm, Joyce always had, and has, a knowledgeable sounding board; she feels less alone. Even so, getting the business up and running was far from easy.

Acquiring the cottage was one thing; transforming it into strikingly unusual business premises another. When By Storm came into existence in May, 1993, the £50,000 renovation and refit of the cottage was still several months off. When work on the cottage finally did begin, it proved to be much more extensive than Joyce had anticipated. The building had to be stripped back to a complete shell. Even the floors had to be removed. The supposed rebuilding schedule of eight weeks also proved wildly ambitious. In the event, renovation took nearly eight months - from September, 1993 until April, 1994.

However, working from a room in a friend's house, Joyce and her sole employee, machinist Irene Harvey, were already hard at work, creating the first By Storm collection. It was an ambitious, and important project for them both because they knew that what they produced, when exhibited, would set the authoritative stamp on the house style. It would make or break the company. It was not a task for the faint-hearted, but in "head hunting" Irene (who is now the company's factory manager), Joyce had made a shrewd choice. She and Irene were an excellent team. Having worked together in Bairdwear, they had developed a close rapport on styles, and Irene could follow Joyce's thinking when creating the samples, a most important attribute.

By August of 1993 they had put together a collection of ninety garments, split into nine separate ranges across the fashion spectrum, from cruisewear to evening wear. Many of the fashions bore the style which is still the distinctive hallmark of By Storm: Soft colours; uncluttered, classic styles; lots of drape; pleated skirts; co-ordinated effects and heavy use of non-crush fabrics. Then it was off to the National Exhibition Centre at Birmingham for the company's debut at the important Premier Collections Exhibition.

The trip was an unqualified success. At the show, a young marketing company from Manchester started chasing them, asking to be allowed to take the By Storm collection to the Far East. Joyce was disinclined to give permission because the marketing company was, itself, in its infancy. However, she eventually agreed the collection could go to Singapore in October. The result from that marketing exercise was a £70,000 order for 2000 garments, right across the full range. In wholesaling terms, for a company in Joyce's market, it was the equivalent of a small football pools win. Individual orders of up-market ranges from independent fashion houses seldom top

£5000.

But fulfilling the massive Singapore order, both by its composition and deadline (which was brought forward to coincide with a new store opening), landed the fledgling By Storm with considerable difficulties. It was still operating from a friend's home, now having spread to two rooms. The long-awaited cottage premises still rang to the builders' heavy tread - although, towards the tail-end of filling the order, By Storm gained much needed access to its two ground floor rooms.

In addition to the inevitable disruption to the company when it flitted to its partially completed new home, there were other difficulties. In wholesaling, the normal procedure for a company after an exhibition is to collect in all its orders, order in the fabric in one large consignment, cut it all in one batch, then have the material run up in as long production runs as possible. This effects economy of scale and cuts out duplication of processes. To fulfil the Singapore order, however, By Storm was forced to carry it out, virtually piecemeal. Involved were several separate small "lays" and production runs because the client had ordered right across the range in small quantities. The average was about two dozen of any style, in two colours. Swamped by the sheer volume of production, By Storm also lost out on other lucrative UK orders totalling about £20,000 which it was unable to fulfil. "The only people who made money on the Singapore order were the agents, who got their commission," says Joyce. "If my partner hadn't helped out we would have been in a lot of difficulty in filling it. But we got it out on time. It also tided us over until we fully opened here."

But if profitability on the Far East order was non-existent, there were other, less tangible rewards. What the order did do was establish strongly the By Storm name within the rag trade and win it a lot of publicity. The exhibition, plus the Singapore order, gave the company genuine credibility as a design house which had its finger on the pulse and knew what would be popular with more exclusive retail. On the back of that collection, the company went on to pick up £15,000 worth of orders from Australia.

Being dropped in at the deep end of the rag trade is no novel experience for Joyce, but the roller-coaster start to wholesaling her designs did underline some of the ever-present difficulties. In wholesaling there is an unbearably long hiatus between payment for completed work and the initial concept. It runs to seven or eight months. Joyce enumerates the process: "In wholesaling first you have the expense of marketing. A stand at an exhibition can cost £3000. You take your orders, but these aren't due to go into the shops for six months. Then, if you are lucky they will pay you in 30 days. You are talking about a minimum of seven months with no money coming in, not to mention the time you've already spent designing and making your collection. In that time you've got to buy your fabric and pay your staff. Sometimes the shops don't even exist when you get round to delivering them their orders."

In contrast, high fashion retail sounds a much better option. To begin with, the mark-up per garment is considerably higher because there is no middleman involved. To make approximately the same turn-over, a design house has to produce and sell only half the number of garments it would have to make as a wholesaler, thereby making considerable savings on outlays for material. Cash returns are also more immediate.

With the long-awaited opening of the cottage, evocative of a bygone age with its antiques and warmly feminine decor, Joyce intended that By Storm would have the best of both worlds. Her idea originally was to continue wholesaling and use the shop as a retail outlet for "extras" run up on specific lines. Within a few weeks of opening, however, she was forced to re-evaluate that strategy. The tail was wagging the dog.

Her stock on the rails was being snapped up, and requests for made to measure styles were beginning to flood in. Within months, following very considerable, and positive, TV and print media coverage, Joyce had taken on two more full-time staff to cope. For the time being, everything was under the one roof; the upper floor was used for retail, while on the ground floor staff worked flat-out producing garments. There was just one problem: They were working flat-out trying to keep up with the made to measure orders being generated by the shop. Bowing to the inevitable, Joyce allowed her business to be market-led, and concentrated on retail. She says: "The retail side took off so quickly that we had to review the situation. We haven't discounted wholesaling, but at the moment we are consolidating on retail. We are opening a shop in London's West End this year. It's just a toe in the water, but we will see how it goes. It's really a destination shop for English customers who don't travel up here."

While all her styles sell well, Joyce is particularly in demand for special occasion wear, very often slightly informal mother of the bride outfits. Bridal gowns, too, are a major part of the made to measure business. To meet customer demand, the company has already expanded, moving all its production staff to a factory ten minutes away in Maryhill, a move which has allowed it to turn the whole of the cottage over to retail sections and a design consultation room. By Storm now has on its books a total of some 15 full-time and part-time staff, about a dozen of whom are based at the factory.

However, there are perils of which Joyce is aware. Having a retail outlet in an affluent suburb of Glasgow has meant that her catchment area of clients tends to be from too narrow an age spectrum for comfort. Most are in the 40 to 50 years age group, while Joyce's aim is to appeal to the 20s right through to the 70s with her designs. As the "local shop" there is also a danger that the area can become over-saturated with her styles, lessening their exclusivity. For that reason, she says she would like to open only one other shop in Scotland - probably in Edinburgh - and establish concessions abroad.

"I don't think I would want more than two shops in Scotland because we're a niche market in a small country," she says. "You are still much less likely to get the same outfit from us than you are going to one of the international fashion houses, but exclusivity is important."

Being faced with a full order book in made to measure is a nice problem to have, but Joyce is still looking to wholesaling and the world's export markets for major company growth. The pull of her styles' appeal is considerable. Clients regularly travel up from England to purchase outfits, and she has clients from Majorca, Australia, the USA and the Far East. To properly enter that market, though, will mean a new By Storm collection being marketed abroad.

One unusual opportunity for building up exports to the USA and Japan is already available for release, once the necessary market research has been completed - a relaunch of the world-famous Paisley Pattern. The Paisley shawl, with its famous burgundy colours and feather-like "teardrop" motif, was a 19th century phenomenon, exported around the world at a time when the town enjoyed the reputation of being one of the world's most prolific, high quality weaving centres. Paisley shawls have turned up in the most unlikely places, from Patagonia in Peru to the prairies of the then New World of North America. Unknown to today's general public, though, is the fact that the Paisley Pattern is just one of literally thousands of wonderful designs produced by the weavers of the time. Locked away in municipal archives, unseen for well over a century, is a huge array of pattern cards, drawings and samples. A handful of the original patterns have been woven on old-fashioned looms specially recreated in Paisley Museum. But the vast majority of designs remained in storage, antique curiosities gathering dust.

Last year Joyce was commissioned by Paisley Museum to update the collection, translating some of those unseen designs into a more modern idiom. From the archives Joyce chose some early Japanese inspired designs, filled with untypical, delicate colourings in soft creams, greens and lilac. The same designs were screen printed onto silk, while others were translated into knitted cloth. By Storm manufactured them into an exclusive collection for the museum. This year, however, the company is creating a full range of silk scarves in the new designs for export.

To anyone visiting By Storm, there is about it a strong flavour of the popular TV serial, House of Elliott, a period drama of the life and times of a young fashion house created by two sisters forced to make their way in the world. The lay-out of the cottage, with its homely, non-businesslike settings and upstairs, downstairs sales areas, reinforces that impression. But there the comparison ends. In its first full year of trading, By Storm achieved a turn-over of £250,000. It has a healthy order book, has made many important expansion decisions and is now fairly firmly entrenched in the UK fashion scene. If all goes well, two or three years down the line, it may be one of a very select band: A young independent design house which has grown an international customer base, without having had to leave Scotland.

THE career of Lex McFadyen, founder of Lex McFadyen Design, Glasgow, in some ways parallels that of Joyce Young. Born in Glasgow, Lex, 37, was also brought up in Ayrshire in the village of Symington, near Prestwick. Educated at Prestwick Academy, at the age of 18 he enrolled at Glasgow School of Art where he studied Fine Art and took as his specialist subject sculpture. His principal interest was working in life classes, but, also like Joyce, he found himself being roped into the school's annual fashion show, which he enjoyed. It was, however, very much a peripheral interest at that time.

His move back to Glasgow as a teenager in the late seventies was accompanied by a somewhat uncanny experience. At the time, finding suitable accommodation in the city wasn't particularly easy. After sharing several flats with pretty mixed results, he came back to the family home in Symington to announce in triumph that he had found the perfect flat in Glasgow's Renfrew Street - only to discover, to his amazement, that 20 years earlier his parents had lived in the exact same tenement, No 224. "It was a Prisoner of War club, which my mother and father ran," said Lex. "They lived above the PoW club, which was a reunion spot for people who had been captured during the war. When I moved into the tenement block, the developers were still in the process of converting it into flats. I'd actually been staying there three months, when I went down to the basement one night to see what was left of the old club. There, lying in the middle of a corridor, was a postcard addressed to my parents. It had been lying there for 20 years having been delivered a few days after they had moved out."

Realising that it was well nigh impossible to follow a career based on his arts qualifications, on graduation from arts school, Lex enrolled at Jordanhill

College to gain a teaching diploma. On completion of the year-long course, he didn't sit his finals but went to Paris for five months to work in a fashion house's retail outlet, not as a designer, but as a general member of the staff. He thoroughly enjoyed the continental interlude but came back in the Autumn to take his final resit examinations. After successfully passing them, he returned to stay with his parents and for a year taught evening classes at Ayr Technical College. On nights off and during the day he also worked in a number of pubs.

For Lex, such jobs were very much stopgap employment as he cast around for something more interesting. In 1982, he found it. He was appointed community arts co-ordinator to run Maryhill Arts Centre in Glasgow. An urban aid project, the centre in Malloch Street was run under the umbrella of Strathclyde Regional Council. Although just 22, Lex proved to have a real talent for the job. Under his leadership, the centre became one of the liveliest community arts projects in the city. As an administrator, Lex found himself heavily involved in planning and financial management, putting together the funding packages which allowed him to develop the centre, widen its range of artistic activities, and take on additional staff. At one point he had a staff of 12, employed under MSC funding and other funding "cocktails."

It was a five-year interlude which taught the young designer a great deal about man management skills and the nitty gritty detail of juggling budgets, balancing accounts, making financial projections and fighting his corner for grant funding. On the arts side, the Centre also honed up his organisational skills. It twice took part in the Edinburgh Festival Fringe, ran a music festival and held workshops in everything from ceramics (it had its own kiln) to dance and drama. Of that period, Lex says, "I enjoyed it - it was a nice level of the arts to be coming in at, being community based. It was very good for me and I picked up a lot of management skills during the time I was there. It certainly gave me a notion to run my own business."

In 1987, after leaving the Maryhill post, he opened his own shop in Albert Drive, on the south side of the city, selling casual and day wear. The switch to becoming a designer was not as dramatic as might be supposed; more a form of evolution. While at the centre, Lex had become involved in designing both fashion wear and stage costumes. He was one of a group of eight talented young city designers who put together a Glasgow Style exhibition for Amsterdam, and had also designed avante garde fashion for top hair stylist Taylor Ferguson, who was beginning to regularly stage international shows. When he opened the shop, Lex also took garments from a number of the designers who had participated in the Dutch show. What he established, along with another girl designer with whom he shared the cost of the premises, was in essence a small Scottish designer group. But the venture was not overly successful.

The siting of the shop had been largely dictated by their modest finances. For a fashion retail unit, the location was poor. There was little passing trade. Indeed, the principal benefits were that the shop could be secured on a cautious annual lease, and that it lay roughly equi-distant between the two principals' homes in the west end and south side of Glasgow. There was no budget for advertising, so Lex was reliant upon word of mouth among the fashionable young set to spread the news of its existence. With Glasgow Style consciousness at its height, Lex believed - perhaps somewhat naively - that clients would seek him out for his more adventurous styles. In the event, they didn't - or rather, they didn't in sufficient numbers to justify his presence there. It would probably have been different nowadays, when with an established client base and a well-known name as a designer, customers would have sought out his premises, irrespective of location. But that was not the case in 1987. He was still relatively unknown. After a year Lex moved to Cook Street, just off the city centre - and out of retail. While still doing a fair amount of made to measure work, which he enjoyed because it strengthened his design concepts, Lex was being pushed more and more in the direction of wholesale and manufacturing. "There was no retail side. We did small runs and one-off dresses for a variety of shops. We did design right across the board. I did the design and cutting myself, and we had a couple of girl machinists," says Lex. "I particularly chose not to involve myself in manufacturing. It didn't really interest me and there are plenty of CMT firms (cut, make and trim) around. I liked variety."

Even so, it was difficult to maintain that stance commercially. A month would go by, and Lex would find the company had done 80 jackets and 50 skirts, or perhaps 20 bomber jackets, to the exclusion of as much design work as he would have liked. It was one of his last big orders - for 120 stylish shirts - which pulled him up sharply and made him re-examine his reasons for coming into the rag trade in the first place. It wasn't to become a manufacturer. After more than three years at Cook Street, he decided to relocate in Old Dumbarton Road in the west end, to concentrate on exclusive dress hire - a route which he saw would ensure his activities were firmly bedded in design.

It was a shrewd move. While in Cook Street, Lex had already established that there was a thriving market in dress hire. City centre hire shops were buying two and three one-off dresses from him a week. As designer and maker of such dresses, he was obviously far better placed than they to create a range of exclusive fashion outfits for hire direct to the public. Coupled with made to measure work from his regular clients, he would have a business whose core activity would always lie in design.

At designer level, dress hire is not cheap. Rentals are £60 per function, a not inordinate sum for a £300 outfit which has a hire life of just five outings before being withdrawn from circulation and placed on the For Sale rail at a price well beneath its original retail value. For their money, though, the ladies get from Lex McFadyen Design what they desire above all else: Guaranteed exclusivity. Every outfit the company creates is a genuine one-off; no outfit is repeated in different colours of fabric, or even in different sizes. If your heart's desire on the hire rail is a size 12 fit and you are an ample size 14, you will have to pass it by to find something in your own range. If the reverse obtains, however, and the dress - as they say in the trade - is "too generous" it will be taken in.

But the exclusivity remains. "That's very important," says Lex. "It can be very embarrassing if two women turn up at the same function in the same dress. I remember one client telling me about the time she went to an important business function in an exclusive restaurant. It was a very high-powered affair, involving a dinner party of about a dozen. She arrived to discover the waitress was wearing the same dress as she was. She spent most of the evening waiting for someone to ask her to go and get them some drinks."

Because of their look and exclusivity, Lex's hire dresses are extremely popular. It is not unusual for a customer to "advance book" the purchase of an outfit while waiting for it to come to the end of its hire life; others, having worn an outfit once as a hire, decide to purchase it outright there and then.

In the hire business, as in any other, there are additional costs to be borne, like scrupulous dry-cleaning of every outfit after each outing. Unusually, Lex does not insist upon large deposits up front as a guarantee against possible damage (hire dresses are simply not insurable). Most clients, Lex finds, treat outfits with great care, although there have been the inevitable mishaps. The most common is not, as one might suppose, cigarette burns, drinks stains or the occasional ripped hem; it is staining of fabrics by certain types of deodorants. If the damage is irreversible, and the outfit warrants it, the company sometimes will replace the damaged bodice with a new one to extend its hire life. But that is only done if the garment, in other respects, is in top class condition and is at the beginning of its hire cycle. Inevitably, choice of fabric for hire dresses tends to be durable as well as top quality. Delicate chiffon and silks are not used because they are so easily damaged. Too close proximity to even a hot radiator can be enough to ruin them.

While distinctly seasonal in volume, there is a rather neat commercial symbiosis between the hire side of the company and its made to measure work. The hire business, which accounts for around a third of the turn-over, pulls in a large number of customers who come to check what is on the For Sale rail. The For Sale rail, in turn, allows the design house to experiment with certain fabrics and colours on designs - knowing that, even if the completed outfit doesn't fit in with the hire range, it will go on general sale, justifying its production. The throughput of hire customers also results in additional made to measure work for special occasion wear from cocktail evenings through to weddings.

Indeed, bridal wear is one of the company's specialities. It designs bridal gowns at an average cost of £1,000, although prices can go as high as £2,000, depending upon the intricacy of the work involved. "A pearl encrusted dress here will cost you £1,800 but in most shops it would be £2,500," says Lex. "You are paying for exclusivity. If we were doing them for retail, they would have to sell for £3,500. There's a limit to how much work you can take on, but all the girls involved with me here are more than machinists. They are fashion graduates from Glasgow School of Art; you are getting a feedback from them, too."

For a designer whose work has been exhibited widely in the UK and abroad - he does all the Taylor Ferguson shows, which have taken him to Paris, New York and London - Lex McFadyen is very much an individualist. He has turned down many offers to design for mainstream, mass market retail. "I've met several companies up here and politely backed out," he says. "A few years ago a leather company asked me to put together a collection, which I did. When the saw it, they said, 'It's not very commercial. Could we just have something with a big collar?' ... 'You mean like all the ones that you've already got?' I asked, pointing at what was on the shelves. They didn't need me; they already had what they wanted."

After a four-year absence from wholesale, Lex recently took a winter range collection to Dusseldorf, Europe's premier show, which created interest among Japanese buyers. He doesn't yet know, however, whether he will follow it up with a visit to Japan later this year with a portfolio. "It's not necessarily what we need as a company. I have to remind myself exactly why I am doing this," he says. "I tend to do a lot of things not for good business reasons. I do it because it's enjoyable. A lot of it isn't financially driven."

The Dusseldorf trip, although heavily subsidised, was still a major expense, but Lex reckons it will pay for itself over the piece, in terms of publicity and in orders generated. At the show, where floor space cost him £160 per square metre, he picked up a contract - ironically from a small chain of independent retailers in the North of England, which he is following up and handling personally. He is also preparing a special video to be sent out to selected retailers, which again he will follow up personally. How far Lex will go down the wholesaling road, though, is debatable. As ever, his interest is in design rather than other commercial aspects of the rag trade.

As Lex sees it, in Scotland manufacturing companies are playing it safe, making middle of the road commercial wear, because it is less of a commercial gamble. "Very few people are pushing design, although there is a huge area of the market which isn't middle of the road," he says.

As a veteran of the Scottish design scene, he believes that the country will only truly make its mark in the world's international designer markets if enabling authorities put their financial muscle behind schemes which will provide long-term momentum. He says: "Dusseldorf is the largest show in Europe. but you need to push into it three and four times before you succeed. Success comes from showing there several times. The people who pick up orders are those who already have German agents who have been working on their behalf, setting up customers and guiding them to their stands. In Scotland there is also a great need for some sort of infra-structure to handle follow-ups between shows. It all comes back to finance and infra-structure. Over the years, there have been smidgens of support, but nothing long-term which links us into the international calendar."

An overly simplistic dream .. or is it? There is no good historical reason why the industrial city of Dusseldorf has emerged as Europe's premier fashion event, save excellent transport links through its international airport, and a will on the part of the authorities to make it happen. Neither does Milan immediately spring to mind as a city steeped in haute couture; most of us think of it in terms of the car industry. The geography of the world is littered with examples of annual world events hosted in the unlikeliest of places. Is it too much to hope that Scotland, even living in the shadow of London, could not host an annual fashion exhibition to push it onto the international circuit?

Anyone around during the time that Glasgow Style burst upon the fashion scene could not have failed to note the flowering of self-confidence among the population. There was a vigorous hopefulness about it all. It would seem that as a nation we only blossom when we see ourselves reflected positively through the eyes of strangers. But can we do it on our own? As far as designer Lex McFadyen is concerned, the jury is still out.

CHAPTER NINE

Importing a brand new culture

E VEN in these cosmopolitan times, amid the increasing homogenisation of society, one of life's most difficult commercial ventures is to attempt to graft one nation's culture onto another. It is a seriously uphill task. There are a variety of reasons for this. Chief among them is that influencing a nation's ingrained habits and attitudes is exceptionally difficult. Ask any Government and it will tell you that persuading the public, say, to adopt more healthy eating habits is a gradual process. Progress tends to be numbered in decades, rather than years. To truly shift our national mind-set on just about any lifestyle pattern requires massive financial investment in long-term, "hearts and minds" strategies amounting to millions of pounds - frequently to achieve only a fractional shift of the compass.

In the moulding of new patterns of behaviour, it would be fair to say business and commerce have met with greater success than Governments. That is hardly to be wondered at, given that the rationale behind commerce is, by and large, to give the public what it wants, at prices it can afford. Being market-driven, ground-breaking commercial developments follow fairly natural progressions; Governments tend to be running against the grain, trying to impose more artificial goals.

Geographic and cultural boundaries are regularly breached by the big invention, such as the arrival of electricity, the combustion engine or, in today's world, the micro-chip, revolutionising our working and leisure patterns. On a slightly lesser scale, so too has the switch from service to self service retail. 'One-stop' convenience shopping has given us malls, hyper-markets and super-stores (all American imports). We queue up at check-out counters in a way undreamed of 30 years ago. Even more docilely, we are prepared to shop at catalogue shops - another foreign import - where, on the basis of photographs, we buy expensive goods without ever seeing or physically examining them. Such an odd concept would have been laughed off Britain's High Streets a decade ago, yet today catalogue shops are a profitable, integral part of everyday commerce.

But direct retail is one thing, culture another, when dealing with nations which have an exceptionally strong sense of their own identity. Business enters into that particular arena at its peril. Disney, arguably the most successful organisation in the world in transcending cultural and language barriers, came to grief over its Euro-complex in France, which, though soldiering on manfully after several relaunches, has been treated with icy Gallic disdain. In another example, Kwik-Fit, the Scottish-based multi-national tyre and exhaust giant, despite all its internationally acknowledged expertise, found the Auld Alliance counted for nothing when it twice tried to establish a foothold in France and twice failed. It was forced to retire from the field, vanquished, having taken a bruisingly expensive beating running into millions of pounds.

However, there have been successful cultural "implants," most notably in the food and drink leisure sector. Outside of their countries of origin, Scotland is probably the most knowledgeable nation in the world on Pakistani and Indian cuisine. Italian and Chinese restaurants abound as do the ubiquitous fast food franchises, imported from the USA. All have been assimilated into Scottish culture. At the gourmet end of the market, up-market hotels have a fine selection of international cuisine with which to tempt diners and in the drinks sector, a myriad range of designer beers and continental-style bistros and theme pubs are an important adjunct to city night life. In fact, in some of Scotland's trendier watering holes it is easier to purchase a bottle of Red Stripe lager than it is to buy a locally made drink.

The Scottish palate, in most respects, is reasonably adventurous - save one. In a country notorious for its sweet tooth (per capita, we consume more sweets, chocolate biscuits and highly sugared cakes than just about anywhere in Europe), we produce some of the foulest, stodgiest, heaviest cakes in existence. Fine baking is a lost art domestically, and a dying one, professionally. In a nation of some five million souls we support only a paltry 350 craft bakers, a select and diminishing band of men and women who uphold the tastes and textures of non mass-produced breads, rolls and cakes. If anyone doubts the claim that traditional Scottish home baking is as dead as the Dodo, the proof is to be found at any church social or coffee morning: On display are pathetic, wizened scones whose acidity scorches the tongue; misshapen pancakes; leaden carrot cake; equally heavy, and overly tart ginger bread; overdone shortbread. Such affairs produce a preponderance of crude slabs of crunched up biscuits glued on top with toffee and melted dark chocolate and a sprinkling of hundreds and thousands; scrunched up balls of breakfast cereals similarly adorned; over-egged or sickly yellow plain sponges; and heavy chocolate gateaux that would not discredit a Highland Games shot putt event. As for good short crust pastry, forget it; it no longer exists.

Into this desert of the spirit, like an angel of mercy, in November, 1989, came Patisserie Florentin, bent upon changing our lowbrow tastes for Scotland's universally awful baking - with superb cakes lovingly prepared from imported French ingredients at the hands of a genuine French epissier who had spent years mastering a craft which borders upon being an art form. What Michelangelo is to painting, so epissiers are to the baking of sweetmeats.

If the reader notes a certain lack of objectivity on the part of the author in the above, let me frankly place my cards upon the table. French baking is the finest in Europe, and at its very pinnacle is the art of the epissier, designing superb, feather-light confections of fresh fruit and custard tarts, sundry tartlets with different fillings, and all manner of pastries. Usually small family concerns (in which inordinately large numbers of relatives appear to be employed), patisseries are to be found on virtually any reasonably sized square or boulevard of every French town, proffering a quite wondrous selection of beautifully prepared cakes, along with croissants and fresh breads. They are an indispensable part of French culture, at the very heart of the civilised ritual of partaking of morning or afternoon coffee at a boulevard cafe and watching the world go by. Patisseries' products sustain the cafe society which is so much a part of France's daily routine. If ever they were to suffer the fate of Scotland's rapidly disappearing craft bakeries, there would be riots in the streets of Paris.

In Scotland, where there has been no real tradition of cafe society since the 19th century, four years ago Patisserie Florentin, the creation of Scots-born Lorna Pellet, 28, and her French husband, Freddie, 31, boldly set out to revolutionise the country's eating habits.

As revolutions go, its beginnings were a trifle on the small side. The couple's first shop, slightly off the beaten track in Thistle Street, Edinburgh, was tiny. With just 180 sq. ft. of rented space at their disposal, Lorna worked "front of the house," selling patisseries over the counter to customers, while at the rear in a minute galley kitchen measuring just 80 sq. ft. Freddie laboured up to 16 hours a day, and eventually seven days a week, producing a daily parade of French cakes from one small oven. Despite the cramped conditions, his confections sold like - well - hot cakes.

Prior to opening, there had been no advertising campaign to alert the public to Patisserie Florentin's existence. Indeed, the only indication of its presence in that backwater street, just off Hanover Street, was its gay, yellow frontage. Yet from the first day of trading, Patisserie Florentin was an immediate success story. As if by magic, a regular clientele, drawn from surrounding offices, materialised at the cake counter. They bought everything in sight. The first three days were a complete sell-out - a regular occurrence in the months to come. As the American, Ralph Waldo Emerson, once observed, if a man should build a better mousetrap - or in this case a better cake - even though he lives in the wilderness, the world will beat a path to his door.

Today, four years on, the world is still beating a path to the door of Patisserie Florentin, though in much changed circumstances. It has moved away from its cupboard-like origins and has now established one of the capital's most popular bistro-style eating places in St. Giles Street, just off the Royal Mile, in spacious premises which ramble pleasantly over three floors. At Stockbridge it has a cafe-delicatessen; and in Leith a full-time bakery servicing the two outlets plus some 18 other restaurants and hotels. It is also in the process of opening another restaurant beside the Lyceum Theatre. When the new restaurant opens, collectively the various establishments will employ between 60 and 90 staff, dependent upon seasonal fluctuations. However, like all true revolutionaries, bent upon grafting onto Scottish life one of the better elements of French culture, the most ambitious project of all still lies ahead ... the couple's plans to franchise Patisserie Florentin throughout the country.

In preparation for that development, which is probably some 18 months to two years from fruition, the company is currently restructuring its administration systems. Patisserie Florentin has come a long way in a remarkably short period of time. Yet one of the strangest aspects of it all is that originally neither Lorna nor Freddie had any intention of starting such a business. It actually came about in the most casual fashion - arising out of Freddie's hatred of Scotland's dreadful cakes, and in particular, Black Forest gateau, which friends used to serve up to the couple on social occasions.

Before Patisserie Florentin was born as a business concept, the couple's lives were heading in a completely different direction.

The daughter of a music teacher, Lorna was brought up in impoverished circumstances in Broxburn, West Lothian, Her parents had separated when she was just six years of age, leaving her mother as the family breadwinner. With two daughters and a son to support, that wasn't easy. Money was tight. From her earliest years, Lorna can't recall a time when she wasn't working to earn herself some pocket money, doing paper rounds, leaflet deliveries and turning her hand to anything which earned her a little cash. "I even took on my brother's ironing for a fee, and did his washing," she recalls with a smile. "But he sacked me. I think he realised that, in paying me, he wasn't left with any pocket money for himself."

The break-up of her parents' marriage, however, affected her quite deeply, and as a consequence of it, she believes she has a fear factor much lower than other business people. "You're not frightened of anything because you have already gone quite far down - you already know what the worst can be," she says. "I'm quite fatalistic in life. Being poor, though, hasn't left me with any scars. I think it gives you a real zest for life and it makes you very appreciative of good things when they come along. It also makes you sensible about money; you don't fritter it away. I think, as a person, you are aware of not having money - and also of having it. However, I am not a person who is driven by material things."

At 15, Lorna took a Saturday job in a bakery shop, a move which was to set her eventually on the road to a vocational catering course. At that stage, though, she had no firm idea of what she would like to do. At Our Lady's High School in Broxburn, she describes herself as a very unmotivated student, doing the bare minimum to pass exams. Her only real interests were music and gymnastics. "I was uninspired except on the sports ground," she admits. "I didn't like the way teachers taught. I didn't really make any connection with education."

Nevertheless, she emerged from the system with a clutch of three or four Higher exam passes. Casting around for a career choice, after checking through the portfolios of various courses, she settled upon a Hotel Catering and Management course at Queen's College in Glasgow on the grounds that it was multi-faceted; its variety of subjects meant she would not be corralled into too narrow a sector of studies. In the event, in her third year, she was to fail her HND certificate exam. Having gone down in accountancy, she point-blank refused to do a resit. "Passing or failing wasn't going to make a blind bit of difference to me getting a job," she says. "I knew I'd get one. I didn't feel that studying over the summer for a resit was necessary. As far as college was concerned, I felt I had done my bit."

However, her three years at Queen's College were far from wasted. While she hated class study, she loved summer and mid-term placements and discovered she had a real passion for hotel and catering work. Of being employed in top hotels like One Devonshire Gardens and trendy pub restaurants like Babbity Bowsters, in Glasgow, she says simply: "I loved it all."

Lorna was also eager to start her own business. In her second year at college she wanted to start up a business from the flat, supplying home-made roulades to delicatessens, but her flat-mates firmly quashed the idea. In her third year, she decided she wanted to start up a staffing agency. It was an idea with some potential. The catering trade is a business sector with a large, transient workforce. Staff turn-over tends to be extremely high. For a modest outlay of around £5,000, and with a detailed knowledge of the trade's requirements, Lorna planned to set up and run an agency which would tap into that large market. During her final year at college, she researched the project, and when she returned to Edinburgh to live with her mother, continued to investigate the idea. Then fate took a hand. Working at Edinburgh's Carlton Hotel as a waitress, she met Freddie, who was a pastry chef at the same hotel.

His background was considerably more cosmopolitan than that of Lorna. Educated at a private school in Lyons, he was a fully trained epissier. With plans to work on a cruise ship - whose on-board fare is legendary for both its frequency and quality - he had come to Scotland to spend a year learning English. At the Carlton, the two struck it off. Romance blossomed and at the end of the time he had allotted to improve his language skills, Freddie elected to stay on in Scotland.

While they were dating, Freddie used to complain about the poor quality of Scottish cakes, but Lorna didn't fully appreciate the gulf which existed until, on her first visit to France with Freddie, she encountered its national institution, the patisserie. She was dumbstruck.

"I just stood there looking and said, 'Wow!'" she recalls. From that moment onwards, all thoughts of establishing a staffing agency vanished. All she could think of was introducing into Scotland Freddie's expertise in making French pastries and cakes.

It was not an entirely new idea. There already existed in Scotland a franchise of French-style cafes which imported their wares direct from France. The crucial difference, however, was that the doughs and mixes were prepared on the other side of the Channel, then brought over to be baked in local ovens. The couple's idea was in many ways a great deal more straight-forward and cost-effective; they proposed to import the raw ingredients, and, using Freddie's skills, bake product from scratch in their own oven.

With a £10,000 legacy from Freddie's father, who had recently died, the

The Next Generation

couple had the necessary start-up capital for such a venture. After sourcing an import supplier in Glasgow, who could buy the wheaten flour, glazes, special French chocolate and other ingredients required direct from the Paris food market, the couple took a two-year lease on the Thistle Street shop. The site had been chosen with some care; although slightly off the main thoroughfare, it was still very much in the heart of the city centre professional business sector, with a good catchment area of offices.

From the start the couple paid a lot of attention to the patisserie's appearance. Its distinctive yellow shop frontage was matched inside by mottled yellow walls and a dado with gold lights, set off by matching curtains at the window. There were good reasons, though, why considerable attention had to be paid to decor. The shop had to look the part. For all its tiny size, Patisserie Florentin was operating at the very top end of the market. Governed by the pricing logistics of short production runs and imported raw ingredients, its cakes retailed at double the price most Scots expected to pay. At a time when most folk routinely paid about 50 pence for a cake, the shop was charging £1.

Occasionally, customers would jib at the cost but Lorna would very quickly set them straight. "To an extent we felt hesitant about the prices," says Lorna. "They were the most expensive cakes retailing in Edinburgh. But my attitude was that the restaurants were charging £2 or £2 50 for such cakes. A lot of people buying from us were taking the cakes home for dinner parties, so I was trying to set the retail prices along those lines. We did have battles with customers unused to paying these prices, but they were fairly low-key affairs. I just explained the reasons for them."

Two things above all Lorna loved about the business - her direct contact with customers and the instant results whenever a new line was introduced. She said: "I built up a great relationship with the customers, and that empowers you. It imbues you with more energy and drive. You start to ask yourself, what else can we do ... I also liked the instancy of the business. You literally could introduce a change in a day. If you introduced a new line, or a different shaped cake, by the end of the day you could see the money in the till as a result of it. There were tangible results to any changes. It was very immediate and very satisfying."

Initially, the shop sold only cakes. Then biscuits, and occasionally chocolates, were added to the lines, and finally croissants. From the local fruit market the couple obtained seasonal fruits, which provided many of the cake fillings. Indeed Patisserie Florentin's company motto is, "Les meilleur produits au rythme des saison." (The best products are in rhythm with the seasons.)

For Freddie, however, the workload was enormous. Opening from 8.00 am to 6.00 pm, six days a week, and eventually seven, the patisserie's complete range of merchandise was being produced from a single oven. Very little could be baked in simultaneous batches. Freddie had to be on the premises up to 16 hours a day, preparing, then baking each individual line. That process was both cumbersome and gravely restrictive on output.

In addition to selling direct to customers, a number of restaurants, impressed by their product quality, were also purchasing the patisserie's croissants and cakes for their own businesses. At one point, Lorna had to curb the wholesaling, which threatened to absorb their full stock. She says: "I remember having an argument with one restaurateur who wanted to buy our products for his place. We said No. He got quite upset when we turned him down. In fact, I had to go round a number of outlets telling them we couldn't supply them any longer. I told them we wanted to give the goods to customers rather than to other businesses. They couldn't believe it, of course. But it had never been our intention to go into wholesaling. We never sought them out; they always came to us."

A year into Thistle Street, the production side improved dramatically when the couple leased premises in Leith, which they fitted out as a proper bakery. It both solved, and added, to the challenge of development. Still working on his own, Freddie began his baking shift at 2.00 am. Lorna would then go down to join him and take the fresh product up to the shop in time for opening. The arrival of the bakery proved something of a logistical problem in terms of transporting goods to Thistle Street. More importantly, though, it threw into sharp relief its severe limitations. With production solved, and extra capacity available, it was becoming increasingly clear that Thistle Street had reached its selling plateau. Its size precluded having two sales personnel behind the counter and expansion was out of the question. Six months before the lease was due to expire, the couple moved in a sales assistant to run the shop, freeing Lorna to prospect new premises.

The site she selected was St Giles Street. Formerly the premises of an Edinburgh law book publishers, the new property seemed, in Lorna's eyes, to be ideal. Spread over three floors - basement, ground and first - it lent itself to phased expansion. Just as crucial was its location, a step or two off the Royal Mile. With everything going for it, this time the couple bought the property.

"Here we are slightly off the beaten track," says Lorna. "I think that part of the attraction to cafe society is being close to, but not on the main street. The building also had a lot of character, which was what we wanted."

Unlike Thistle Street, here the premises had a surfeit of space for the patisserie's immediate requirements, and the couple were financially cautious in its development. Indeed, as a fallback, they always thought that, if necessary, they would rent out the upper floor area if it proved surplus to their needs. In the event, they probably erred rather heavily on the side of safety. The new Patisserie Florentin began with a retail sector, selling cakes and croissants, a small cafe section of eight tables serving cakes and coffee, and an Espresso bar. These proved an immediate success and very quickly the couple built up a somewhat eclectic and colourful clientele.

"It was a wonderful mix. We would get a lot of lawyers coming in - and their clients. You would have the legal profession down one side and the crims down the other," said Lorna. "There were nurses coming on and going off shift; students; out-of-town visitors and of course tourists. At different times of the day the whole complexion of the place changes because the various groups tend to come in at different times."

Within 11 months of opening, the couple refurbished the upstairs section and opened a bistro selling savoury meals in addition to their normal bakery products. To give the business a lengthier selling window, the opening hours which started out as 8.00 am to 6.00 pm were also extended to midnight.

Of the restaurant development, Lorna says: "We started with soups and salads, and pates. When that went well we just gradually built it up, producing new hand-written menus as we went along. You had people coming in and sitting down so you had them captured for a bit longer, so that gave you an opportunity to sell them something else."

The success of Patisserie Florentin's St. Giles Street flagship, however, cannot be laid solely at the door of exclusivity of its products. While high quality, authentic French baking not readily available elsewhere may bring customers through the door, what keeps them coming back is the way the company markets itself. It does so in a highly individualistic manner. That is worth examining in more detail because, in the catering sector which Patisserie Florentin occupies, standing out from the pack in Edinburgh is probably a more difficult feat than in any city in Britain.

As the United Kingdom's premier tourist destination after London, history and commerce walk hand in hand in Edinburgh. The city centre abounds in quaint pubs which simply reek of character and bygone charm. Moreover, a goodly number of them provide very excellent pub grub, attractively displayed and served to lunch-time crowds and beyond, since many of the public houses possess all-day liquor licences.

From the outset, Lorna's instinct was to walk in entirely the opposite direction. As a matter of policy, Patisserie Florentin does not sell alcohol at its St Giles Street premises. "This had to be a place where I would feel comfortable coming in as a woman on my own. Although it's different in Glasgow, in Edinburgh we didn't have a market where people would come out to a cafe on their own," she explained. "I also wanted children to be able to come here, because I think kids should be able to go anywhere and be welcome to run around, with staff just guiding them back to mum when necessary. We refused to contemplate serving alcohol here. In fact, not serving drink has had a positive effect upon custom. We've created our own niche."

Warming to her theme, she continued: " Alcohol would completely change the character of the place. Even in the friendliest of bars it is very difficult for me, as a woman, to go in on my own. Because there's alcohol present, there is an association; people think they have a right to approach you. You feel threatened. A lot of women feel exactly the same as I do. Anyway, drink shouldn't be forced down folks' throats. They should be able to go into an alcohol-free, non-threatening environment. We want everyone to feel they can come in here on their own at any time of day or night and feel absolutely safe."

Having so closely defined the market, flowing from those decisions were certain natural concomitants. Non-threatening, alcohol-free environment also meant non-threatening decor. The ambience of Patisserie Florentin had to be comfortingly casual, yet still fairly avante garde and interesting, with a free-flowing artistic flavour. In that, the couple were immensely helped by a complete overhaul of the premises' interior design and a new company logo. Given her own past artistic interests at high school, that task normally would have devolved to Lorna but for the intervention of a regular customer, a young girl designer who told her: "I know exactly what you need." In all truth, she did. From her selection of ideas, came the true identity of Patisserie Florentin.

In Thistle Street, the couple's logo, required by them to put the company stamp on products such as boxes of chocolates and jams, had been a map of France, with a tiny dot to indicate the town of Lyons, where Freddie had trained, which is regarded as the nation's gourmet capital. It was not a success. The general public hadn't a clue what the logo meant. They were so geographically challenged that they didn't recognise the contours of the map of France, far less realise the significance of the town being highlighted.

The new look, however, was strong and assertive. Drawn from the predominant yellow colours of the frontage, it had at its core a central motif of sun flowers. Even the curtains, sourced and imported from the USA, carried a sun flower design. The cafe, too, evolved in decor, with the emphasis on a casually unfinished, but attractive look. The over-all effect was highly visual, but homely, where the eye was constantly alighting on something new, be it a detail of a robust modernistic oil painting or other decoration.

Lorna is no doubt the changes - and the new logo - have contributed considerably to the company's success. She says: "Some companies have decent logos, but very often it depends upon how you stamp it around. In our case it has been an important factor. So has the decor. We wanted a place in which people felt comfortable. When I worked in One Devonshire Gardens in Glasgow I loved the seduction of it, but hated the formality of the setting. I just don't think that's what eating out is about; I think it compensates for the food, and eating out should be about the food. Actually, I think it's a lot harder to do decor casually well than to do it in a formal style."

With its oddly shaped rooms, and a fairly steep staircase sweeping up to the first floor, Patisserie Florentin's layout is not exactly a conventional one. Most traders would be concerned at the fairly large amount of "dead" square footage lost to passageways and stairs. However, Lorna and Freddie have turned its distinctive appearance to good account. The premises divide quite naturally into three public areas, each with their own particular clientele. On the ground floor is a small non-smoking seated area and the cakes counter; and across from it, with its own entrance from the street, a coffee bar for smokers, again fitted out with a sprinkling of tables. On the first floor, surprisingly spacious and with good natural light, is the restaurant. The over-all effect is a place with something for everyone, where customers can feel truly relaxed and be themselves, whether they are in on their own for a coffee and a cake and a read at the paper, or meeting friends for a casual lunch. Open some 16 hours a day, it has become one of the city centre's most enduringly popular haunts - with not an alcoholic drink in sight.

In April, 1994, Patisserie Florentin spread its wings a little further, establishing a retail shop and small cafe in North West Circus Place, Stockbridge. Oddly enough, the development came about, not because of the popularity of its cakes, but because Patisserie Florentin was selling so few of them. Lorna said: "There was a delicatessen there which was taking just four cakes a day from us. We couldn't believe a shop could sell such a small amount of our product, so when the opportunity arose we bought premises in Stockbridge. It was just a hunch, but we were proved right. There was public demand for our cakes in that area."

Since moving out of Thistle Street, the couple had always contemplated opening another retail outlet. Stockbridge was something in the nature of an experiment. With just eight tables, its principal business lies in over the counter sales. But plans to develop it along the lines of St Giles Street have proved impossible. To Lorna's considerable frustration, development has been hemmed in by commercial restrictions. The couple were refused permission to paint the frontage in the Patisserie Florentin corporate colour, yellow. They wanted to open the shop until 10.00 pm, but have been restricted to 7.00 pm opening, despite a petition signed by a thousand local people favouring longer opening hours. They were also refused permission to increase the number of tables. A fairly vigorous battle, fought out in the columns of local newspapers, has failed to have any of those restrictions lifted.

In one way, though, Stockbridge has been a complete success. Taken as a piece of market research, it proves that the market for patisserie product is there. Lorna also views wholesaling to restaurants and hotels in much the same light. She says: "We are breaking new ground in Scotland. If we are selling product to other organisations, it means our cakes are becoming more socially acceptable; they become part of people's diet."

It is perhaps natural that a company like Patisserie Florentin, with its sights set firmly on the finer things of life, should gravitate towards the arts world, which provides a fair sprinkling of its clientele. In recent years, during the Edinburgh Festival, in a special marquee erected at the Mound, in the grounds of the National Gallery, it has catered to Festival visitors attending art exhibitions - creating an extremely high profile for itself. This year it intends to extend the marquee's opening hours virtually to a 24-hour service.

In a further incursion into the arts world, the company is also opening a new restaurant in Grindlay Street, next to the Lyceum Theatre. Open from 8.00 am until midnight, the restaurant will depart a little from the normal Patisserie Florentin formula, in that it will serve wine. With 60 covers, one of its principal missions will be to cater for visitors who find that they are hungry during the afternoon "graveyard" hours, when most restaurants are shut. "During the day it will be very relaxed. Customers can come in and have just a snack or an out of hours three-course meal," says Lorna. "In the evening it will be a little more formal and upmarket."

Until the present, Patisserie Florentin might be said to have grown organically. More formal systems, though, are now having to be introduced in preparation for the next leap forward, franchising. The company has been going through a period of consolidation. "1995 has been one of the most boring years of consultancy," says Lorna. "We took on a human resources company which instituted staff psychology questionnaires. We've been re-organising staffing and an infra-structure which will manage franchising. Until now, our systems have always come just after we have done something, and that has been compensated for by a lot of hard work. But franchise has to be much more formalised. We're going in for overkill - introducing a part-time personal assistant, an office manager and a production manager for the bakery to network all the systems. We've also created a post for an operations manager. Over the next two and a half years we should have five franchises on the go. We have already got our day to day manual, which will go out to every franchisee. The franchisee will also keep a daily log so that both of us will have a complete diary of everything that is happening."

With a young family to raise, Lorna has cut back her day to day involvement to 25 hours a week. "Motherhood is the most important thing for me," she says. "I've had to become a lot more organised. Coming in for shorter hours, I actually find I'm getting through more work. Because everything is fresh, I'm probably more focused on what I'm doing. Monday to Thursday, I come in up until 2.00 to 2.30 pm. I also delegate more work than I used to."

At the bakery, Freddie now has a full complement of staff, all of whom he has trained personally. The patisserie still gets the bulk of its ingredients through its Glasgow importer, but from time to time phones France direct in search of specific lines from individual manufacturers' catalogues.

"When we're on the phone and tell them in our pigeon French that we're a patisserie calling from Scotland, they just burst out laughing," says Lorna, with a grin. Perhaps the fame - or more accurately, ill-fame - of Scotland's home produced cakes has gone before us.

But Patisserie Florentin is here to stay, in a bold venture to re-educate our national palate. A lot of us sweet-toothed Scots, starved of top-flight, authentic French confections which are just a dreamlike memory from an occasional holiday across the Channel, are devoutly thankful for its existence. It is probably too much to hope for a Patisserie Florentin in every major town in Scotland. But I do, I do.

CHAPTER TEN

Profits versus freedom

BY definition, a business that is not going forward is going backwards, even if it is merely standing still. Like the shark, which from the moment of birth requires to be in constant motion for the remainder of its life just to breathe, commercial concerns require year on year development and expansion. The yardstick by which we judge whether enterprises are successful or otherwise is monetary. We measure them off in turn-over and profit. Yet paradoxically there are successful businesses that are not driven by the financial ethic. Profit, beyond a certain basic level, is secondary to other goals. All the founders require from the business is a living - and the freedom to get on with their lives in other directions, without becoming excessively shackled to the clamant demands of capitalism.

Such enterprises we call lifestyle businesses. And they are the dream of many a man and woman, stuck, for purely financial reasons, in stultifying or unsatisfying jobs. All life is compromise. But given that it - so far as we can ascertain from this side of the veil - is not a dress rehearsal for anything else, many of us aspire towards a lifestyle that fulfils us emotionally and professionally, while offering us a reasonable degree of financial security. The route to personal independence normally lies down one of two paths. The first is the capitalist way, based on acquisition. By building, or excelling in business, people arrive at a comfortable nest-egg which after a lot of foot slogging, allows them from a vantage point of relative wealth and status, to broaden their horizons and indulge their earlier dreams. For them, having money behind their hand represents independence. In truth, many travelling that route never ever make it back to their original goal. The pull of business is too strong, personal financial obligations keep rising and all of us have a habit of living up to our incomes, whatever they may be. As John Lennon once wrote: "Life is what happens to us while we're making plans."

The second route to personal independence is to decide that money doesn't matter. Earning only sufficient for their basic needs, people can lead rich and full lives because they have engineered for themselves the space they need to follow their grand dreams and passions, usually in some form of highly creative activity.

Let no-one imagine, though, that it is easy. Living outside the system never is. It requires high levels of commitment, resourcefulness and self-belief. In one of those odd quirks, to create and sustain a lifestyle business often needs more - rather than less - acquired skills in marketing, promotion and salesmanship than when working in the business mainstream. There is no organisational back-up; people are dependent upon themselves for all their resources, from book-keeping and secretarial administration to publicity and marketing. Another major factor is also at play. Commerce thrives upon continuity. Maintaining and broadening the width of business contacts is essential for growth. Those running lifestyle businesses, however, being more intent on reserving their time for their own activities and creative interests, do not immerse themselves fully in that milieu. They dip into the market place sporadically. Thus their client base tends to be narrow and slow-growing because the engine of progress is driven by creativity rather than profit-making considerations. Lifestyle businesses generally lack normal commercial momentum. To a considerable degree, the people within them find they are jumping the same hurdles repeatedly. That they can, and do, prosper sufficiently to sustain their way of life in modern times is often a triumph of the human spirit. To put it at its simplest: Lifestyle businesses are extremely hard work.

One couple who have developed a successful small business which permits them the freedom to pursue their artistic interests are applied artist Fiona Allardyce-Lewis, 32, and her life partner, Andrew Weatherhead, 30, a ceramic artist, who live in Moniaive, a tiny community nestling in the beautiful, but remote fastness of the Dumfries-shire hills. From a century-old stone smithy - little more than a farm outhouse - Fiona creates on wood hand-painted designs and figurative work for sale across Britain and further afield. Vibrantly coloured, and immensely detailed, the scenes she depicts are often humorous, slightly bawdy but always appealing. The items she paints range in size from tiny, postage stamp size framed mirrors, small triptychs and wooden candleholders to decorated chairs, large screens and even specially commissioned 40ft. murals.

Most of these unusual and original compositions - destined to become the craft antiques of the next century - can be found on sale in exclusive shops and Fine Art galleries from London to Edinburgh. Fiona has also notched up an impressive number of exhibitions of her work at venues which include the Victoria & Albert Museum, London; Birmingham's The Angle Gallery; the Society of Scottish Artists at the Royal Scottish Academy, Edinburgh; the Edinburgh Arts Club and many others. She has also staged a private showing for Prince Charles.

Meanwhile, nearby the smithy in another outbuilding, her partner, Andrew, spends his days designing superb, hand-crafted and decorated pottery, using metal oxides to create the meticulous designs and scenes, painted free-hand in single brush strokes directly onto the pieces before a final firing. From his kiln emerge fine examples of the potter's art to grace quality galleries and Fine Art studios. The two activities ideally complement one another in the small visitors' gallery, housed in one section of the smithy, which is devoted to displays of the artists' work.

Andrew's arrival as a fully independent potter within the workshop is a fairly recent development. It has taken six long, hard years for the business to evolve slowly to the point where its future looks assured. How the couple got there involved a very considerable amount of self-sacrifice, which fairly clearly delineates the difference between the dream and the reality of living on the fruits of artistic creativity.

Born in Aberdeen, Fiona spent most of her childhood in East Africa. The family emigrated when Fiona was just three months old to Uganda where her father, John, had obtained a job building swimming pools, before becoming a teacher in agriculture. One of a family of three, she was to live abroad for 12 years in Malawi and Uganda until it became too dangerous to remain because of the depredations of Africa's Black Hitler, the dictator Idi Amin. "I can remember him coming to our English language school one day," Fiona recalls. "He made us all wear woolly dresses and skirts on a really hot day and just about everybody fainted. I was about eight at the time. My dad used to play rugby against him sometimes. Although Amin loved the Scots, he was a real schizophrenic personality, and we moved a couple of years after he came to power."

Following the family's return to Scotland, her father eventually obtained a post as a maths and science teacher at a school outside Biggar, Lanarkshire. Fiona attended the local Biggar High School. It was there that she met Andrew, the beginning of a school romance which was to become a permanent relationship. Education, for Fiona, proved difficult, but not because of the cultural change of arriving back in what, for her, was a foreign country. It was discovered, when she was 16, that she suffered from dyslexia. Transferring from Biggar High to the dyslexia unit at George Watson College, she remained there until she was 18, gaining Higher English and Art, and three Ordinary level passes. Exams, for Fiona, were always an intimidating feature. Because of her condition, she had a scribe who took down her answers. Also present was a personal invigilator to ensure examination conditions were maintained. "It was quite nerve-racking, all of us crowded into the one small room," she says. "But I did manage to get a B pass in English. I was accepted for Glasgow School of Art as part of the 10 per cent of students they take in on the strength of their portfolios."

Andrew, meanwhile, had gone to Dundee to study ceramics, a career parting of the ways which meant the two only saw each other at weekends.

In Glasgow, Fiona's original ambition was to become a book illustrator, but there were no art school courses available in the subject, so she took a Fine Arts Honours degree in printmaking, graduating in 1987. Obtaining employment, however, was difficult. When a round of applications to city print studios, seeking technician jobs, failed to produce a career opening, she worked as an independent artist out of the WASP studio at Trongate. For Fiona, it was a less than satisfactory arrangement because virtually the whole of her graduation year was also working at WASP. It was like an extension of art school at a time when she felt she should be branching out, exploring new influences other than her peer group. At the studio she produced figurative etchings, which she candidly admits were unsellable because they were so gloomy. Her subject matter, she believes, was heavily influenced by a period working as a care assistant in the hospice of an Edinburgh old folks' home, while still an art student. "It was horrendous," she laughs. "I was very into producing etchings of withering hands and feet. It wasn't anything anybody would want on their walls."

A year down the line, after a spell of freelance teaching, Fiona decided it was time to get some sort of career going. Her first thought was to set up a print-making and etchings business in Glasgow, but closer examination of the finances involved at a Scottish Enterprise business course for graduates showed it to be an impossible ambition. She and Andrew seriously considered emigrating to either the USA or Australia where they knew their artistic skills could command a good living. In the end, however, they both decided they wanted to live and work in Scotland. The matter was more or less settled when Andrew obtained a job as a potter with a ceramics firm in Dumfries.

By this time, still in Glasgow, Fiona was producing and selling silk screen frames and a variety of other craft items. She was also painting and varnishing wooden artefacts and developing her distinctive, three-dimensional style. The vividness of the colours - a throwback to those she encountered during her days in Africa - and their cheerful ornamentation were eventually to make them popular, saleable items. But taking the plunge and moving to Dumfries-shire to join Andrew as an independent small crafts business was, for Fiona, a "pretty scary" move. "I knew that once I embarked upon it, that would be me for life," she says. "It was Andrew who persuaded me."

The plan was for Andrew to continue at the pottery, bringing in a small but steady wage, while Fiona set up the crafts business with a £3000 low interest loan from the Prince's Scottish Youth Business Trust, a £1,000 Trust grant, and a £1,000 overdraft facility from the bank. She also qualified for a £40 a week enterprise allowance for a year. It took her three attempts, though, to convince the Trust that what she was embarking upon was going to be a viable business. The Trust had reservations over whether her range of product was wide enough. Ornamental mirrors - her first, and at the time, only item - were not going to be a repeat buy, so Fiona was going to require a steady throughput of new clients in a sparsely populated area. However, she continued to press her case, and eventually the Trust relented. With the finance finally in place, the couple rented accommodation in Moniaive, and acquired, for a pepper corn lease, the smithy as a workshop. It took six months to complete its conversion.

In the beginning it was a spartan existence. With no cash available for a car, Andrew had to cycle 14 miles every day to and from his work near Dumfries. In the smithy, which had electricity but no heating, the couple installed a tiny coal stove which made scant impression upon the icy blasts whistling through the building. Even today it is a far from comfortable work centre, but Fiona, hardened by years of working there, seems oblivious to the cold, although she does admit that winters can be uncomfortable.

Fiona's initial idea, when she started the business in April, 1990, was to sell her work locally. She believed that, with its large passing tourist trade, Dumfries would be her principal market. Certainly, in the beginning, that assumption appeared to be borne out. Taking samples round shops and other outlets, her first exhibition was of 40 mirrors, of varying sizes, for a cafe in the town. It was highly successful. Nearly all the mirrors - which represented two

The Next Generation

months' work - were sold. For a year, Fiona persevered, attending local craft fairs and exhibitions and selling to visitors who came to nearby holiday homes. She sold in reasonable quantities, but the financial numbers still weren't adding up. As time progressed, she found herself being required to sell further and further afield. Today, nearly 75 per cent of her work is sold south of the border. Her turn-over has also tripled over the years.

In the early years, when it was a constant battle to pull in enough revenue to pay for the next batch of materials, the couple were fortunate to acquire as a patron a Swedish Count, who would regularly arrive at the smithy to buy pieces. The "casual" visits always seemed to coincide with the arrival of the couple's electricity bill. That long-running friendship has also seen the Count make available to Fiona and Andrew his London home any time the couple travel to the capital on selling trips. "He's been absolutely wonderful," says Fiona. "So, too, have the couple here who have given Andrew the use of stables for his pottery and kiln."

In her opening year of trading, there was one other major development. Fiona sold a lot of her work to the Studio One Gallery in Edinburgh, whose owner, John Johnson, gave her invaluable advice on the types of designs which would prove popular. Equally importantly, she gained a lot of commercial information on prices, mark-ups, and lengths of time she would have to await payment. Fiona very rightly refuses to put her work out to galleries and shops on a sale or return basis, reckoning that outlets will try harder to sell items if they have paid for them. Today she can afford to be fairly selective on where her work is sold, and she is also fortunate in that she has the populist touch: Everything she produces finds a market. "I have never been turned away by any shop I have ever approached. They all have taken my work," says Fiona. Considering how difficult she personally finds salesmanship, that is a quite extra-ordinary feat.

As recognition of her work has grown, she has also been able to charge out her time on a more realistic rate, basing her prices on labour, plus cost of materials. Inevitably, once the galleries have added on their mark-up, it pushes her works of art into the more expensive range of outlets south of the border.

In the beginning, though, despite the interest shown by retailers in her ornamental mirrors, it was a question of trial and error. Even obtaining basic materials was a struggle. Mirrors arrived scratched from local suppliers because they were unwrapped; woods she was being offered from wood yards were unsuitable. However, gradually the "daft wee girlie," by dint of regular visits, established a rapport with her suppliers and now gets excellent service. She still remembers, though, the first time she went in to complain that mirrors were being sent unwrapped. The next batch she received was carefully covered - in old copies of the Sunday Sport, Britain's raunchiest paper. Today Fiona cuts her own mirrors herself, and the woods she uses, normally Douglas pine, she generally seasons for up to six months before use.

It was in her second year that Fiona began to extend her range, moving into the pictorial scenes which have become such a hallmark of her work. Her themes range from perspective drawings of historic buildings to create a three-dimensional effect, to old-style Christmas feasts. Best loved, though, are the impishly humorous, slightly naughty tableaux which can feature anything from a bank manager captured reading the Beano on a decorated clock to a triptych of slightly decadent, amply bosomed ladies eating sweets before moving on to more fleshly entertainments.

That broadening of content was to open the doors of many galleries to her, an important consideration in getting her work known. She even staged an exhibition in her own Royal Bank of Scotland branch in Dumfries, which in return for a decorated wall clock, for permanent display, commuted existing interest on her bank loan - a feat which more than a few new businesses would like to emulate. Another major commission that year was for three 40ft. murals for the Loreburne shopping centre in Dumfries, which helped keep the business ticking over. It was the following year, however, when Fiona achieved her major financial breakthrough. She and Andrew attended a Birmingham craft trade fair. The largest event of the year on the arts and crafts calendar, it is attended by galleries and dealers from all over England and Wales, and in one single show her work was introduced to a wider range of commercial contacts than she could have achieved in a year of travelling around the country. For an outlay of some £700 on materials, publicity brochures (she received a subsidy towards the cost of her exhibition stand and accommodation), Fiona pulled in more than £3,000 of work. "We actually had to close the order book," she says. "I couldn't handle any more."

The Birmingham show also called upon the couple to make a second important decision about the business: It was not going to deal in volume retail. A Japanese buyer, interested in Fiona's slightly risqué work, wanted to commission something like 2000 items for export, but Fiona turned him down. "It would have meant working on that order to the exclusion of everything else," she says, "and I didn't want to do that. Besides, it would have driven me mad with boredom, working on the one picture over and over again. I'm not interested, either, in using stencils to produce the scenes, and hiring people to complete them. That would push me away from what I want to do and into the management of production lines. I didn't want that at all. It was a very conscious decision not to go that route, and I've never regretted turning down such a big order. There are more important things than money."

If the Birmingham show was a watershed in the development of the business, it was also the event which laid down the foundations of her working pattern. Built around a framework of the exhibitions which she will stage across Britain during the year, Fiona today tries to plan out her work schedule over 12 months. From January to April most of her time is spent concentrating on making new exhibits and items for sale during the British crafts fairs season. When that slackens off, she undertakes private commissions, which comprise a fairly substantial proportion of her work, then in the latter part of the year she works hard to produce material for the Christmas rush. "You try to work three or four months ahead of delivery," she says. "It takes a bit of juggling. I try to fix all the exhibitions first so that I can fit in everything else around them."

Inevitably, the business continues to evolve and change, including her target markets. More of her work than ever before is now aimed at Fine Art galleries, where clients are accustomed to paying retail prices ranging between £100 and £600 for her work. The price tag includes a hefty mark-up by the galleries, which is why her work finds a readier sale in England than in Scotland. It is also one of the reasons why, this year, she will be cutting out the middle man to sell direct to the public at the UK's most prestigious crafts fair which rigorously selects the artists who apply to exhibit at it. "I'm really looking forward to the fairs, because it is an opportunity to be alongside the best in the country. It will also allow me to sell my work nearer to the prices I want to charge," she says.

The trade fairs will also be an important showcase for her partner Andrew's ceramics. Since becoming a full-time independent ceramics artist just two years ago, he has been slowly building up a following for his work. Like Fiona, he has gone down the route of participating in numerous exhibitions, so far confined to Scotland and England. While an excellent method of getting an artist known, the venues often don't offer on the spot sales. The three craft fairs will give him the best commercial platform yet to gain widespread UK public awareness, as well as enable him, for the first time, to display properly the new selections of hand-decorated ceramic tiles he has added to his range.

The story of Fiona and Andrew is very much one of artistic dedication and steadfastness of purpose. They still lead a lifestyle which most of us would consider extremely frugal. But creeping into the equation now are things which most of us take for granted. These days there is a car outside the door, obviating the need to cycle everywhere. They manage low-rate winter holidays abroad, to Cyprus and Malta, and they reap enormous satisfaction from their work. Who of us would be brave enough to say they haven't got the balance right?

GEOGRAPHICAL remoteness and lifestyle businesses tend to go hand in hand, which is not really surprising. Divorced by distance or difficult transport links from mainstream commerce, fewer opportunities arise for people to establish commercial enterprises. Their activities tend to be embedded in tourism, arts and crafts or working with the land or sea; or indeed, a combination of some of those activities. Few businesses, though, can be more isolated than that being established by Anna Macfie and her husband Shaun. They are creating on Knoydart, one of the last true wildernesses in Scotland, a tree nursery devoted to growing some of the broad leaf species that, all too frequently, have been vanishing from the Scottish Highlands, which in recent decades has been swamped by the proliferation on its uplands of fast-growing pine plantations.

Situated in the West Highlands, beyond Fort William, Knoydart is a vast and inaccessible peninsula pincered between Loch Hourn and Loch Nevis, two sea lochs sweeping into the Sound of Sleat, the narrow stretch of water separating the mainland from the Isle of Skye. It was along this wild coastline, fissured with sea lochs and inlets, that the French allies of the Jacobite rebellion played a deadly game of hide and seek with the British Navy blockade ships before finally spiriting away Charles Edward Stuart to a life of exile, in the cruel months following the failure of the '45 insurrection.

Knoydart has changed little in the intervening centuries. To reach the Loch Hourn Broadleaves nursery involves a breathtakingly scenic journey along a single-track road threading through the great cleft of Glenelg and its spectacular mountains. When the traveller runs out of road, at Arnisdale, a 40-minute journey by open boat across the loch is required to reach destination's end, Cnoc Gorm. On the loch shore side of Knoydart where the nursery is situated there are only three or four isolated houses, with their own generators to provide electricity. There are no roads, save forestry tracks, and phone links to the area were only established a few years ago, a convoluted arrangement involving a switch from land lines to radio transmission from Mallaig. That apart, the mixed blessings of civilisation have largely passed it by.

It is here over the last few years that Anna and Shaun, on a half acre of ground owned by her parents, have been setting about the back-breaking task of establishing from virgin territory a tree nursery. A more formidable enterprise would be difficult to imagine. The initial logistics, alone, were daunting: Every single item, from fencing posts and wire, peat, agricultural and nursery equipment, domestic fuel and provisions had to be brought in by boat. That was only the beginning. Fences had to be erected to keep out the red deer, then the ground had to be drained, cleared and broken up. Initially, the couple had to tackle that task with spades. Later they acquired a rotovator, which helped considerably, but there is still a large element of heavy manual labour.

Clearing and creating seed beds from bracken covered ground involves ripping out by hand a dense matrix of roots which lie up to 2ft. below the soil. As if the terrain is not enough to contend with, the couple also have had to endure the most unlovely denizens of the West Highlands, the clouds of voracious midges which infest the countryside. In the season, when their numbers are at a peak, their maddening bites can even stampede cows in a frenzy of discomfort.

For Anna, though, coming back to Knoydart to establish a tree nursery was a return to her roots, and she was fairly inured to attacks from such insect predators. The eldest of three children, Anna moved to the area with the family when her father, Peter Carr, a fisherman, made his home on Knoydart 20 years ago. Growing up as a young girl amid its beauty and quiet solitude left an indelible impression upon her. For her it has always remained a place of special importance, an unspoiled wilderness which during her formative years was hers to explore and enjoy in all its seasons. No-one who has not grown up living in such close, and lonely, proximity to nature can truly understand the bond which is formed. It is a uniquely personal link, sifting out life's irrelevancies, and marking one's soul; a communion, if you will, between the land and the person.

However, it had never been Anna's original intention to return to Knoydart to establish a business. Studying on her own at home, because there are no schools on Knoydart, she achieved Higher exam passes in English, Art and Biology. It was enough to gain her entry to Edinburgh Art College, and a sociable life in the Capital with friends she made within the students' co-operative movement. In 1991, at the age of 24, she graduated as Bachelor of Arts in painting. For Anna, the six years she spent in Edinburgh were an enjoyable and creative interlude, but following graduation she wanted to become involved in something different. Already having an interest in horticulture and tree planting, she gravitated fairly naturally into conservation work. A mix of both paid and voluntary work saw her become involved in countryside management, tree planting and fencing. Tree planting and seed gathering projects throughout the West Highlands during 1991 and 1992 took her on two separate trips to the Hebridean island of Rum (where the midges are the most infamous in the Highlands), a number of other locations and back to her beloved Knoydart. As her interest in the work deepened, she enrolled for several part-time courses covering such diverse subjects as running a tree nursery handling a chain saw and woodland management. By this time she was seriously entertaining the thought that she could establish a tree nursery of her own.

"I think I became aware of the conservation picture slowly," she says. "I was on Rum doing some voluntary work for the nature reserve, picking holly and alder, and I enjoyed it so much that I thought this was something I could do for myself. My parents happened to have a bit of land, so I went straight back there from Rum and asked if I could use it. They agreed immediately. They have always been tremendously supportive."

By the Spring of 1992, the die was cast. Moving back to Knoydart on a much more permanent basis, Anna began planning her tree nursery business in earnest. To raise the necessary start-up capital, she first approached Highlands and Islands Enterprise. No-one could doubt her determination. To get grant information she crossed the Sound of Sleat by small boat to meet up with its representative at Ornsay in Skye - only to be pointed in the direction of the Rural Enterprise Programme located at Loch Carron. A little later she also made an approach to the Prince's Scottish Youth Business Trust. Organising her business trips to see the two organisations tended to be a somewhat lengthy process, involving long journeys by road through Kyle on the post bus, then the regular bus service to Skye. However, they were eventually to bear fruit: Anna received from the Trust and Rural Enterprise a total of £3,000 in grants to start the business.

Three factors helped considerably in clinching the outcome. Firstly, Anna had amassed a considerable amount of practical knowledge in her chosen field, having worked with and studied tree nursery operations; secondly, she was proposing to launch the business at a time when it was something of a growers' market. Perhaps in response to the long-running public backlash over "tax break" pine afforestation, and additional incentives for broad leaf tree planting, there was a much greater interest in repopulating estates with a much wider variety of trees. The third reason was that Anna, who had identified Knoydart and Skye as her target markets, had received from the then management of the Knoydart estate, in response to her market research, an exceptionally positive letter which said it was shortly to embark upon a major tree planting programme which would absorb anything - and everything - her nursery produced. In the event, the estate was broken up and sold off and the new replanting programme has not yet been proceeded with, but at the time it seemed an omen of good fortune.

By this time, too, Anna had met Shaun. Widely travelled, and able to turn his hand to anything, Shaun was very much a citizen of the world, educated in life's university. For the past ten years he had settled in Drumnadrochit, on the banks of Loch Ness, where he worked as a gardener in Glen Urquhart. Drawn together by their mutual interest, romance bloomed. The couple eventually were to marry in June, 1993, but at that time having someone close with whom she could discuss ideas, for Anna, was a wonderful bonus. Shaun's background made him the ideal work-mate and companion.

In September of 1992, when the second of the two grants was approved, the work began in earnest at Knoydart. Purchases of fence posts, wire, peat, peat, pots, tools and equipment were ferried across to Cnoc Gorm in Peter Carr's 27-ft. motor boat. With the help of friends, a deer fence was erected round the nursery area, and drainage ditches dug. A large seed box table was constructed out of fence posts and planted with oak - the extra table height being necessary to prevent mice from eating the acorns. In a sheltered spot, the couple also erected a polytunnel. At £800, it was their single most expensive piece of equipment, and was central to their plans. Under its cover, they hoped to grow young trees, bringing them on and hardening them to have them ready for sale in 18 months, rather than the customary two years. Shaun and Anna spent three weeks drilling post holes and embedding the structure in concrete.

In its benign conditions, they were to raise a fine first crop of birch and other seedlings - only to see their greenhouse wrecked in the first fierce gales to sweep Knoydart. "The plastic cover pulled out of the ground," said Anna. "When erected, the manufacturers only allowed for about 12 inches of the cover to be embedded in the ground along the sides, a really niggardly amount. If they'd allowed 3 or 4ft, it would be standing yet."

Fortunately, the couple were able to salvage the cover intact and are planning to re-erect it after deer-fencing the area and growing a windbreak. "Working in the polytunnel is a wonderful thing," Anna adds. "For a start, it keeps you out of the way of the midges."

The heavy, back-breaking work of preparing the nursery site continued throughout much of that first Autumn. The ground had to be dug out by hand and seaweed physically barrowed up from the shoreline to enrich the soil. While it was highly satisfying to see the nursery take shape, the most pleasant tasks of the year were undoubtedly the couple's Autumn forays through the estate, Kintail and Glenelg, collecting seeds for planting. Rowan, holly, alder, birch, ash, hawthorn and the rarer hazel were all picked, to add to the previous year's stock, which included oak and Scots pine.

In the germination and propagation of seeds, one must forget any visions of latter-day Johnny Appleseeds winsomely leaping through the forest, scattering at their heels handfuls of seed which, in due season, miraculously sprout. Tree growing is a meticulous, at times difficult, business. Anna and Shaun started off with an extremely long list of varieties, hoping gradually to build up a wide range of stock. Every type of seed requires to be treated before being planted - and the treatments vary considerably from species to species. Rowan berries, for example, require to be placed in sand outside for 18 months in a process known as stratifying. Alder seeds need to be exposed to a temperature of minus 5 degrees Centigrade (normal domestic refrigeration temperature) for a period of three weeks before planting; some like holly require a warm treatment, and even then are difficult to grow. From a crop of 10 lbs of berries it is not unknown for professional horticulturists to obtain no more than 20 or so seedlings, a hopelessly non-commercial return for the effort involved. Thus to ensure best growing conditions, a meticulous diary has to be kept on when and what treatments have been embarked upon. Anna also keeps records of seeds and where and when they were collected.

The Spring of 1993, the planting season, found the couple working harder than ever. The workload was eased, in some measure, by the acquisition of two fairly vital pieces of equipment. The first was a second-hand Dacia pick-up, ideal for rough terrain work, and for transportation of peat, phosphates and other materials to the nursery site. At £200 it was no showroom model, but it was worth its weight in gold. The second item was even more important, a £360 second-hand rotovator which was bought from an Inverness tool hire company. Shaun spent 70 hours renovating it, before it was pressed into service, breaking the ground. "It was a wonderful asset," says Anna. "It just cut through long swathes of unbroken turf to produce lovely black earth which would have taken us ages to dig out."

In the polytunnel, peat-lined seed boxes were set out and some nine varieties of trees planted, the principal one being birch. They were eventually to produce a good crop, but that lay in the future. Outside, there was other work to be done, liming out already broken ground, weeding, and rotovating more planting areas. Throughout the summer the heavy schedule of tasks continued. There was water to be piped in to the site from a nearby burn, and large areas of the nursery beds had to be cleared of boulders, ash tree roots and the ever-present tangle of sub-soil bracken roots - heavy, demanding labour which all had to be accomplished by hand. However, the couple were beginning to see the first results of their plantings. In the polytunnel, seedlings sprouted well and were moved out into the open to harden, while the ground inside was rotovated.

Having taken a decision that, where-ever possible, trees would be grown using organic methods, there was also regular weeding to be done, because some tree species, like birch, fail to develop if "shaded out" by faster-growing undergrowth. By the Autumn, more trees had been added to the windbreak being grown near the polytunnel and the seasonal task of collecting more seeds from the surrounding countryside embarked upon.

The most momentous event of the year, however, was yet to come, the birth of the couple's daughter, Rowan, that December. With the arrival of a baby, the couple's routine underwent something of a change. Back living in Drumnadrochit, in a small cottage commanding a magnificent view of the area, the tree nursery had to be tended, long-range, with regular monthly visits to inspect the site and carry out the various tasks required - not a major problem in what is very much a seasonal business. Throughout 1994 and 1995, the cycle of seed collection, seed planting, ground clearing and fertilising of further large seed beds continued. Added to the range of seeds being germinated were wild cherry, bird cherry, blackthorn, crab apple and juniper. However, 1995 was not a good year. Following the Spring planting in two large, and laboriously prepared new seed beds, Knoydart experienced its heaviest rainfall in 20 years. An unprecedented three-week deluge precipitated the couple's first crop failure, an event which can hit even the most experienced of growers. It was followed in summer by drought, which required them to embark upon a programme of careful watering and nutrient feeding of their young trees. As an added precaution, as the drought progressed, the couple left the long grass around the larger saplings to act as a mulch. All survived, but in the seed beds little grew, save the rowan seedlings. Nevertheless, the couple have amassed a stock of some 4,000 young trees for the market.

With the Knoydart estate not proceeding with a major tree-planting project, the challenge now for the couple is to build up alternative markets. To date, they have been selling in small volume batches of different species, principally through word of mouth. However, they are in the process of prospecting the possibility of setting up a marketing co-operative for small tree growers, such as exists in the North of Scotland.

"There is actually an advantage in there being a number of small nurseries in the West Highlands," says Anna. "The main problem facing the small grower is growing enough of each species. If you are trying to supply a woodland grant scheme you need thousands of each species, and you never know what you are going to be asked for. If it's for a piece of soggy bog it could be alder or willow. Or on a nice bit of fertile ground it could be oak, hazel or wild cherry. On your own as a small nursery, you have to have a wide range. But selling to a growers' co-operative a business like ourselves could supply half of the order required."

Having experienced at first hand as a student in Edinburgh the effectiveness of co-operatives, Anna believes it is a system which has much to commend it to Highland growers. Another commercial route she and Shaun are considering is specialising in hard-to-grow varieties of trees, which are always in demand and command three to four times the price of more easily raised species. They have been closely following new growing methods of holly being pioneered by the Forestry Commission.

"It's an environmental niche which is very worthwhile and it's one in which we are becoming more interested," says Anna. "I think if trees like holly, crab apple and rowan are fruiting they very quickly create a change for the better in your wildlife and birdlife. In barren places like Knoydart that can make such a difference."

Whatever path the Loch Hourn Broadleaves nursery goes down, the one certainty is that it will require from the couple continued commitment to build upon the hard work already invested in creating, within a wilderness, a small, but viable nursery. Like nearly all lifestyle businesses, it has been a long time in the growing. But then so are trees. In the next century a lot of visitors and residents within the Highlands will have cause to be grateful to young couples like Anna and Shaun who have helped repopulate its landscape with the natural beauty of indigenous trees which bring in their wake a resurgence of the plant and bird life we have been orphaned from for far too long.

CHAPTER ELEVEN

Good psychology wins customers

THERE are certain universal constants in successful business. One of them is an ability to read human nature and to be aware of how people are likely to react in given situations. The business which uses basic psychology to correctly position itself in its market place reaps long-term commercial rewards even when times are lean.

The most salutary lesson I ever learned about the lasting commercial value of correctly analysing your psychological market place was from an open air Egyptian trader, while on a trip to see the pyramids on the outskirts of Cairo.

From a visitor's perspective, the outing left much to be desired. It was hot and it was dusty on the historic site. Far from being edifices awash in timeless mystery and romance, as portrayed in countless films and travelogues, the pyramids sit, disconcertingly, on a patch of desert beside a multi-lane modern highway, all but enveloped by Cairo's urban sprawl.

Emerging, blinking, into the sunshine, from a most perfunctory inspection of the Cheops Pyramid, many tourists headed like homing pigeons for a small open-air market selling the usual range of souvenirs: Egyptian hieroglyphics on papyrus; leather belts; T-shirts; decorated cotton bags and a wide range of ornaments and trinkets. Annoyed at having long-cherished illusions shattered, and having had such a thoroughly disappointing experience, I checked out the prices but bought nothing. From the market, I looked down the hill, perhaps half a mile, to where the tour buses were parked not far from a restaurant, awaiting our return.

To one side, was another open-air market. Much smaller than the one near the pyramids, it comprised no more than three or four stalls, and appeared to be run by a single trader. After meandering down the steep, dusty path towards the coach, I had a look at the goods. They were precisely the same as those being sold at the top of the hill.

I asked the trader to give me a price on a T-shirt, which turned out to be a good deal more expensive than I expected. Preparing to haggle, I protested: "But they are selling the exact same shirts at half that price at the market up the hill."

The trader replied quietly: "Go there."

In two words he had completely undermined my bargaining power. We both knew there was no way I was going to clamber back up the track to the other market - even if I had time to do so before the tour coach departed.

It is worth analysing a little further that trader's calm certainty that he had judged his market absolutely correctly - a certainty made all the more impressive by the fact that he was able to uphold premium selling prices at a time when Egypt was suffering from a disastrous tourist slump.

All around, businesses were slashing prices, desperate to get at least some through-put of revenue. Yet here was a sole trader so confident of his market position that he could continue to command top prices for his merchandise in a dramatically contracting market. By the simple expedient of being absolutely last in the queue of vendors trying to sell to tourists, he had established trading exclusivity - and by definition a strong niche market.

He was a shrewd student of human nature. He knew that most coach parties operated on tight time schedules; he was prepared to let visitors run the gauntlet of traders on arrival - banking on them being more interested in seeing the pyramids than in bargain hunting; he was prepared to let the market on the hill have first call on them as they emerged from the pyramids; but he also knew a fair number, hot and in need of cool refreshments, would quickly make their way down towards the buses along with others, still undecided on purchases. When they did, his stalls were the last opportunity to buy souvenirs.

From the teeming streets of Cairo to the pleasant environs of the university town of St Andrews in the Kingdom of Fife may seem a fairly extra-ordinary leap, but if it is, it is only one of geography. Commercial principles know no boundaries. Establishing a "psychologically sound" business is just as valid in Scotland as it is in Egypt. A quite compelling illustration of that fact is the successful bicycle business of Spokes.

The Next Generation

Now completing its third full year of trading, Spokes was set up in 1992 in South Street by Craig Grieve, 24, and his life partner, Caroline Corcoran, 25. From a standing start, in three years, in what is very much a specialist market, it has completely dominated its niche. The turn-over figures speak for themselves. In the first year the business grossed £60,000; last year the figure reached £130,000 and in its current financial year it is heading for a £200,000 turn-over. Because it is a business which mirrors perfectly the attitudes and habits of the town, fitting smoothly into its lifestyle patterns, Spokes will always be a success

Yet it was a business towards which Caroline and Craig gravitated virtually by default. The young couple, who have been together for five years, and hail from the small Fife village of Windygates, were pushing in a completely different career direction. Only when Craig failed to make progress in his first choice of occupation did they re-examine their joint skills and abilities - and set about founding the cycleshop.

Both had attended Fife College. Caroline completed a three-year course in accounts and business studies while Craig undertook a course embracing media studies and leisure management. A keen sportsman and cyclist, Craig's intention was to work in local authority leisure centre management, but he failed to find a post. Caroline was more fortunate. She worked for several companies, including being a hire negotiator for a plant hire firm.

Meanwhile, Craig, a former Scottish junior cycle internationalist, continued to concentrate on his cycling hobby, going on training runs five nights a week while still seeking employment. Sick of not having a job, he decided to do what he knew best - and go into the cycle business.

There were certain in-built advantages in his decision to turn his sporting hobby into a business. As an enthusiast of many years' standing, he knew better than most the intricacies of the cycle world. He knew what serious cyclists required; he had practical experience of cycle components and their technical specifications and performance. At his finger-tips was a very considerable wealth of knowledge about all types of bikes, the people who used them, and the fashions and fads of the cycle world. He had a wide range of contacts within the sport, including cycle sales reps, who, themselves, tend to be enthusiasts. At club and sports level, the cycling world is a close-knit community where everyone knows everyone else. As Craig's girlfriend, Caroline, although not a serious cyclist, had been drawn into its world. The couple had many mutual friends who were keen cyclists.

For a brief period, Craig worked for a cycle shop in Leven, and when a branch opened in Methil, he was offered its managership. Instead, he decided to branch out on his own.

The first task was to decide where to set up shop in Fife, a county with a strong cycling tradition, and which, in the North East of the county, is well to the fore in its plans to establish cycle tracks across the countryside. The couple's over-riding instinct was to open in St Andrews, rather than the more densely populated town of Kirkcaldy. There was nothing magical about the choice; it was made for very practical reasons. As a university town, St Andrews has a large all year round student population which in term time numbers between 5000 and 7000. The university's study halls and faculties are fairly widely scattered across the town. The distances involved being quite considerable, about three-quarters of the students rely on bikes as a cheap, simple method of getting around the town.

As St Andrews is situated on exceptionally flat coastal terrain, cycling is also a favourite mode of transport for many other townspeople. The sight of formally attired business gents, cycling to and from their offices, clutching briefcases and umbrellas to the handlebars, is not uncommon. Equally, tweed clad ladies of mature years are often to be found threading their way along thoroughfares. While not as densely populated with cyclists as, say, Cambridge, St Andrews enjoys a surprisingly wide age range of people who regularly use bikes in and around the town. All this the couple knew in fairly general fashion from their own local knowledge. "A lot of people here are pretty environment-conscious," says Caroline. "Cycling has a 'green' image and they like to be part of that."

To test their observations, Caroline and Craig spent three or four weekends, standing on street corners watching cyclists. They talked with many of them - asking what types of bikes they liked and where they got them repaired. They established, too, that in town there was only one other cycle repairer. It was not a dedicated cycle shop, but a small, if long established, ancillary department within a shop whose core business was selling toys. That was the sole competition for the niche market the couple hoped to service.

Armed with that information, the next step for the couple was to raise the capital they needed to open a shop. For that, they turned to Fife Enterprise in Leven which helped them draw up a business plan, then pointed the couple in the direction of the Prince's Scottish Youth Business Trust. Launched by Prince Charles in 1989, the Trust is a special funding and development organisation for young people aged between 18 and 25 years of age. It provides seed corn finance and professional support to fledgling entrepreneurs. The Trust has been instrumental in transforming the lives of many young Scots, giving them the initial financial backing needed to start up their own businesses. At its discretion, the Trust disburses both loans and grants to applicants coming to it with commercially sound ideas. Guided by Fife Enterprise, Craig and Caroline were successful in their application to their local regional Trust panel. They were advanced a total of £7000 - £5000 as a low-interest loan, and £2000 as a direct grant.

Finding suitable premises took them quite some time. The couple wanted to locate near to the town centre, and in St Andrews commercial properties can be difficult to obtain. Eventually, however, they moved into their present South Street address, which was once part of a building society. While quickly growing rather cramped for their needs - bikes and parts take up very considerable space - it was the start that they needed.

In stocking the shop, the couple were greatly assisted by their cycling contacts. Many of the company reps covering the area were already personal friends and were able to give them exceptionally detailed advice about the brands of bikes which were proven popular lines in the area. Equally importantly, their rep friends were able to persuade their own bosses to give the young couple excellent credit terms on their opening stock, a most important consideration.

Bicycles, these days, are not cheap. A reasonable quality mountain bike retails at more than £300. Downhill racers, with their finely weighted aluminium and carbon fibre frames, cost around £1,500. For a racer, which is individually customised by its owner, the serious enthusiast doesn't blink at shelling out £2,500. At any given time, Spokes can be carrying up to £20,000 of stock in bikes, accessories and parts. Against that sort of outlay, the length of credit being given is important. Craig and Caroline, because they were part of the cycling scene, were given the sort of manufacturers' terms reserved for well established traders, rather than the much shorter deadlines afforded newcomers.

"If it hadn't been for the advice and help of the reps, we'd probably have made a great deal more mistakes in the type of stock we ordered," says Caroline. "They kept us right on a lot of things."

"Insider" knowledge of the cycle world, however, is no automatic passport to business success. Craig and Caroline found that other organisations were less accommodating towards novice traders. For a whole variety of services, everyone else wanted their money up front - on the basis that what was financially here today might not necessarily be there tomorrow. On the day the couple opened for business, out of their £7000 start-up capital, they had in the bank just £100.

"We opened the doors not knowing what to expect," says Caroline. "By the end of that first day we'd taken in £150 - and we thought we'd just about covered ourselves."

Initially, Craig ran the shop while Caroline kept on working in her other job, doing the books at home at night, and helping out in the shop at weekends. However, as the business began to grow, she moved into it full-time. Craig still carried out the repairs, but very quickly Caroline also learned how to strip down bikes and do the more straight-forward servicing. Today the shop, which opens seven days a week, employs a full-time bike mechanic on the staff, plus a part-time Saturday boy.

Contrary to what outsiders might think, the cycle trade is not seasonal, but an all the year round business. In January, February and March the big selling items are the costly racing bike frames, wheels and accessories, as enthusiasts prepare for the new season. In summer the trade switches to good quality mountain bikes; then in September and October, as the student population expands, there is a major demand for cheaper versions of mountain bikes. In the run-up to Christmas, a wide variety of brands and accessories are to the fore.

And all the year round, there are repairs. Repairs and accessories are a mainstay of the shop, accounting for about 70 per cent of the shop's work, and contributing about 30 per cent to its annual turn-over. Spokes has been so successful in capturing that market, that the only rival in town has pulled out of the field to concentrate on its principal business. Among the best customers for repairs are students. Vandalism to parked bikes is a regular occurrence, and students who sail effortlessly through honours degrees and doctorates seem to have grave difficulty in effecting even the most basic of repairs. Every week upwards of 50 students pass through the shop doors seeking assistance on everything from altering the saddle height to replacing inner tubes. Because space is at such a premium, Spokes has a policy of carrying out all repairs, either same day or within 24 hours. The shop also insists customers uplift them within 24 hours. If they don't, the bikes are taken into storage elsewhere and customers charged a daily storage rate. It is a wise precaution; it is not unknown for students to put their bikes in for repair - then leave town for several weeks.

Surprisingly, Spokes does not mend punctures; it's too time-consuming to be cost-effective. The spin-off from that decision is that students tend to buy new tubes, rather than go to the bother of mending punctures.

While the business has prospered mightily, the one area which Caroline feels they neglected during start-up was advertising their presence. "We didn't do enough of it," she says. "We placed adverts in the local newspaper and in the student yearbook, but even after all this time we still get local people coming through the door who say they didn't realise we were in existence. In the last eight months we've spent about £1000 in advertising."

In 1994 Spokes added a new sideline to its operations, bike hires for the thousands of visitors who flock into the town during the summer months. The shop now has a fleet of 20 bikes which it hires out at £10.50 a day. Last year it also entered into a deal with one of the major hotels to make hire bikes available.

As the business continues to evolve, one of the most important aspects of its growth has been the decision to stick largely to the quality end of the market. "We can't really compete with the companies volume selling £100 bikes," says Caroline. "They tend to require more repairs while under guarantee than more expensive bikes. For the profit margins involved, it isn't really worth the hassle to our type of operation. Besides, this is an area where a lot of people are looking to buy from the better quality ranges."

With the business now firmly established as part of the lifestyle of St Andrews, Craig has found time to launch in his home village of Windygates the Kingdom Racing Team, a cycle club which boasts a membership of 50. He also feels confident enough to leave the day to day management of the shop to Caroline, while he takes on a cycle rep's job - at the request of one of the manufacturers. "He's happier when he is out and about, rather than stuck in the shop all the time," says Caroline.

It seems reasonably safe to predict that, from Craig's travels as a sales rep, will evolve a second cycle outlet somewhere else in the county when he spots a suitable location. Expansion and evolution is the natural direction of business. The couple have already picked up a business award for the way they have developed their operation. That is hardly to be wondered at. The strength of Spokes lies in its straight-forward practicality - and the ability of Craig and Caroline to make it an indispensable part of the natural lifestyle of rural Fife.

ANOTHER new business based in St Andrews is also enjoying success because it plays to the natural strengths of the county. Golf Quest (St Andrews), which now also trades as Adventures In Golf in an international joint venture, was founded in January, 1991, by Jamie Gardner, 29. It is a travel business which specialises in arranging golfing holidays for visitors to Scotland.

In many regards it is an object lesson on how a profitable niche business can be built upon the back of what might be termed a "world brand." The name of St Andrews is instantly identifiable around the globe as the cradle of golf.

Outside of Wimbledon, there is no more internationally famous sports venue anywhere in the United Kingdom; the Grand National doesn't even come close. To achieve the level of world-wide branding granted to St Andrews by historical chance would require the advertising budget of a Coca Cola or a Nike multinational empire. For a world not fortunate enough to have on its doorstep the spiritual home of golf, it is the dream of every golfing enthusiast to at least once visit and play over the most famous links course in existence. Jamie Gardner's idea was to translate that dream into reality. Using St Andrews as the "brand name," he set up a travel business to organise special golfing itineraries for visitors which would take in not only St Andrews but other fine, if lesser known, Scottish courses.

In launching the business, he was also playing to his personal strengths. He had an intimate knowledge of the area, having grown up in St Andrews. As a youngster, he had caddied for golfers over the Old Course, and he also was familiar with many of the courses throughout the East of Scotland. A keen golfer, playing off a handicap of eight, he knew at first hand the types of events which would interest and intrigue visitors, making their tailor-made Scottish sporting holidays memorable events in their lives.

Jamie's own background was unusual in that he was a member of a Services family. Born in Singapore, he spent his early years being educated in an army school in Hong Kong, before his father, a "civil servant" for the Government's top-secret GCHQ at Cheltenham, obtained a posting back to a Services base within the United Kingdom. In 1972 they moved to St Andrews. Jamie, still of primary school age, attended a local school before moving on to complete his education at Madras College, from which he emerged with six Higher and nine Ordinary-level exam passes. In 1985 he enrolled at Stirling University, where he took a Bachelor of Arts Honours degree in history. During his four-year course at university, he also found time to study economics for two years.

On leaving university at the age of 23, with no clear idea of what he wanted to do, he applied to join the RAF. After attending several selection board interviews, he was told to come back in a couple of years. He was not overly despondent at the rebuff. Analysing the reasons for the postponement, he says: "I decided I wasn't getting very far because my heart wasn't really in it. In career terms, there wasn't anything which really appealed to me. It seemed rather frivolous to continue going for endless interviews."

Coming to the conclusion that he was "unemployable" in the loosest sense of the word, Jamie decided that working for himself was the only answer. To do that he realised he would require finance to set up his chosen business, whatever it might be, and also additional business training. That wasn't as easy as it sounded. In the eighties, today's well-established network of training programmes and organisations geared to encourage new start-ups was in its infancy. Getting information on them was patchy. "A lot of letters kept coming back to me marked, Not known at this address," said Jamie. "I found myself going round in circles, being directed back to organisations which I had already approached."

Eventually, with a certain amount of ironic coincidence, he found himself back at the university he had just left. At Stirling he was accepted for a Scottish Enterprise graduate enterprise programme. Along with some 20 graduates he learned the basics of accountancy and marketing, networking, and even assertiveness role playing. Most important of all, he was given step by step guidance in developing a business plan for his idea of starting up a golf tour company. All the elements of his concept were subjected to extremely practical scrutiny before the final structure evolved. From the foundation course, Jamie emerged with a clear picture of his market place: A range of holidays for golfers coming from outside Scotland, which would be customised to their wishes, and would offer a high degree of personalised service. One of the beauties of the business was that it could be grown organically, as he gained experience. Having worked part-time in many jobs associated with golf, Jamie knew the St Andrews scene extremely well; now he cast his net wider, gathering in data from golf courses within the North East, gaining from club secretaries information about playing times and rates and availability to visitors. He also began building up a data base of information on suitable hotels and bed and breakfast establishments, concentrating very much on Fife and Perthshire - areas he felt, that as a one-man band, he could service adequately.

When Golf Quest (St Andrews) was finally launched in 1991, with £3000 investment capital from the Prince's Scottish Youth Business Trust, Jamie had a network of some 10 regional courses on his books. His initial target was the English market. Advertising in national golf magazines brought him in a reasonable supply of golfing parties. By and large they were looking for inexpensive, but reasonable accommodation in addition to access to courses, which was slightly lower down the scale of operations than he wished to be. But it was a start. He also networked his service through the Scottish Tourist Board, which again brought him clients.

In business - as in golf - timing is everything, and Golf Quest's arrival in the market place came just after one of the periodic shake-outs to which the travel industry, with its strange financial logistics, is prone. Many of the small-time outfits operating at Jamie's level had gone out of business, unable to withstand the twin pressures of recession and the cut-price package holidays being offered by an industry trying rather desperately to keep its cash flow going while awaiting better times. "I started when the market was really low," says Jamie. "Everybody was finding it difficult and there had been a clear-out of competitors."

It was not naiveté on his part. His was a business which at that time dealt with incoming clients only. The volumes of business he was initially dealing with were small, and relatively unaffected by the difficult trading conditions. With no staff, his overheads were at an absolute minimum. In effect, he had arrived in the travel business, lean and hungry, to a fairly clear field. "Every year the market is getting better," says Jamie of Golf Quest, which has now reached a turn-over of £175,000 - about a third of the turn-over of the complete operation he runs.

From the start, Jamie's business philosophy was to offer clients who wished it an extremely personalised service, providing them with everything they required - from hire cars to chauffeur driven limousines. It was common practice for him to meet clients on arrival, see they were properly settled in at their accommodation, double check on their course bookings, then move onto their next venue to ensure everything was up to standard. Unlike some firms offering sports holidays, he also believed in spelling out exactly what would be available to them. If a championship course insisted on golfers having a minimum handicap, as at Muirfield, that information was passed on. If the client would not be permitted to play a particular course unless successful in a daily ballot, as at St Andrews, or if lady golfers weren't permitted to play Royal Troon, clients were told that also, well in advance of arrival.

"I don't believe in telling people just part of the story," says Jamie. "If there are course restrictions on visitors, they should be made aware of them before they come. That way, there is no way people feel they've been let down. There is no sense of disappointment, and they can go on to enjoy a great holiday experience. Everything is up front. Clients are given a complete breakdown of the costs of their holiday and the fees we charge. You have got to have the self-confidence to charge people a decent rate for the job."

That straight-forward approach has more than paid dividends. About 70 per cent of the business generated by Golf Quest today comes from repeat clients or from referrals. Golf Quest regularly gets letters of thanks from delighted holidaymakers. Fairly typical is one from the USA in which a client writes, "Here I sit in sunny Southern California dreaming once again about the wonderful golfing holiday my brother and I shared in Scotland ... the Old Course at St Andrews was, of course, the icing on the cake. Your service was first class and the time you took to cater to our needs was exceptional."

For Jamie, attention to detail is paramount. "You have to know how individual clubs and hotels work," he says. Interwoven into the packages he now organises are link-ups with non-golfing events so that clients can enjoy a completely rounded Scottish experience. This is of particular benefit to couples who may not wish to golf every day, but wish to interlace sport with a large element of sight-seeing.

In the development of Golf Quest there have been perhaps four important milestones; firstly, the company's gradual extension of its booking services to cover the whole of Scotland's golf courses. Today it has approximately 25 recommended courses on its books, with the emphasis on links courses, which foreign golfers don't have available to them at home.

The second big step was the introduction of new computerisation, which improved booking procedures and allowed the company to greatly extend its business data base. Nowadays, from first contact and interview with a client, the business can pull together a completely personalised itinerary - all bookings and prices confirmed - and have it faxed to the customer within 72 hours. Depending on its complexity, the turn-around on itinerary often can be even faster. On acceptance, the client is then mailed the details, along with a comprehensive information package.

From computerisation flowed additional marketing benefits. In the winter of 1993, Golf Quest began producing a four-page newsletter. Entitled Letter from St Andrews, it was written largely by Jamie, himself, and mailed out to prospective clients. It has since been incorporated into the larger Adventures In Golf newsletter and goes out to 8000 addressees on the computer's expanded mailing list. The marketing technique is also interesting. The newsletter very deliberately employs a soft-sell technique. Illustrated with monochrome golfing prints and photographs from bygone eras, in tone it is like a friend's letter dropping through the letterbox, bringing the reader up to date with golfing events within the United Kingdom, and St Andrews in particular. The "homespun" look to it, in marked contrast to the slick, hard sell commercial brochures usually sent out by the travel industry, gives it unusual customer appeal. It appears to be addressing a fraternity of golfers as a fellow enthusiast, rather than as a company. The "branding" of St Andrews is something which rivals can't call upon, either, as a marketing tool.

The third major development was easing Golf Quest into a more upper-range holiday niche, and increasing its prices to reflect properly the high level of service the company offered. It took Jamie more than three years to get the business to a size where he felt confident enough to push it more up-market, which was always his original goal. These days, a fairly typical package will cost holidaymakers £800 to £900. The cost is inclusive of accommodation, green fees, car hire and other incidentals, but does not include the cost of travel to and from Scotland. "It was a case of putting up prices and not panicking if I was losing business," he says. "I was also beginning to think of working with people in the USA. We needed travel agent links and better US penetration."

That came to fruition in 1994, with Jamie becoming the third leg of a joint venture, Adventures in Golf. Set up in the late seventies by partners Ken Hamill and David Patterson, Adventures in Golf was a highly successful "two centre" golfing travel agency. From his base in New Hampshire, Ken looked after bookings throughout the USA, while David, from Northumberland, handled the logistical side of the business. Early in 1994, the partners were looking to establish a presence in St Andrews. Jamie's business was a neat fit. While still continuing to trade as Golf Quest, he donned a second business "hat" - becoming the Scottish end of Adventures in Golf.

The move, at one stroke, opened up major new markets for Jamie and gave him the desired penetration of the USA that he needed. The joint venture has also made possible additional developments which were beyond reach as a small company operating on its own. Under the Adventures in Golf umbrella, Jamie can for the first time contemplate developing a "two way" business, booking Scottish clients on golfing holidays to the USA, and expanding to incorporate similar specialised holidays on the continent and possibly in Eire, in consultation with his new partners.

The Adventures in Golf joint venture, in years to come, undoubtedly will be the driving force in Jamie's company expansion. It has the potential to propel his business to a much higher slice of his niche market, making him all but unassailable by rivals wishing to step into his specialist travel area. Further down the line, that solid trading base may even afford him an opportunity to tap into the large, and extremely lucrative Japanese leisure market, once other business "building blocks" have been put in place.

For Jamie Gardner, the sky is the limit. However, he will continue to run his own business, Golf Quest (St Andrews) in tandem with Adventures in Golf. Having a unique "brand name" at his disposal in his own back yard is something no rival can call upon, without physically establishing a presence in St Andrews.

CHAPTER TWELVE

Survival can be unconventional

FORGET, for a moment, the eternal clash of political doctrines over the dilemma of wealth and poverty. One of the greatest social tragedies of our age is unemployment. It does a great deal more than wreck individual financial security; for those of us accustomed to having staff jobs who find ourselves unexpectedly out of work, and struggling unsuccessfully to find new employment, it eats away like a cancer at the human spirit.

Perhaps the greatest psychological blow which unemployment delivers to our self esteem is a sense of utter helplessness; our professional destinies seldom lie directly in our own hands.

In this chapter, the company which snatched victory from the very jaws of defeat when the original chain which owned the business went into liquidation is called, with considerable aptness, The Outdoor Survival Shop. Perhaps the most unusual feature of its success is that it was achieved by the new owners breaking virtually all the norms of conventional business start-ups.

Most fledgling companies start small, in inexpensive locations. The Outdoor Survival Shop began trading from a plum Glasgow city centre site, with an extremely high rateable value. Just to break even it had to gross more than £280,000 a year. In staffing, it leaped into its market with a complement of five (including the two owners) - again a much higher level than normal for a single frontage shop.

The anomalies continue. For fully three and a half months, the shop doors remained closed to the public as its would-be purchasers strove to clinch a deal with the liquidator. After such a lengthy absence from trading, commercial logic dictates that any relaunch requires a heavy advertising spend by the new management to alert customers the retail outlet is back in business. Again that didn't happen. Cash constraints were such that the shop's advertising budget stretched only to a couple of adverts in two city-based daily papers the day before opening. Indeed, the main thrust of the extremely low-key relaunch involved no more than putting a notice in the window saying the shop was back in business under new management and was running a special Opening Sale.

Just about everything in The Outdoors Survival Shop's initial sales development ran counter to what most professionals would say was required. Yet within one month of trading, the new management had cleared off £16,000 worth of borrowings and was completely debt-free.

How was that accomplished? Let us go back to the beginning - and the day that two staff members of the original company, Survival Aids, heard on the grapevine that their organisation was in serious financial straits. Paul Harrison, 26, and Pauline Wilkie, 25, who were eventually to take over the business, arrived at ownership of The Outdoor Survival Shop in Buchanan Street, Glasgow, by widely differing routes.

An apprentice joiner from Cumbria, Paul - who is known to his friends as Harry - joined the Survival Aids company, which had a chain of 13 branches throughout Britain and also ran a major catalogue. It traded principally in the more expensive, top of the range outdoor gear required by serious world travellers, climbers, hill walkers and outdoor sportsmen and women. If you wanted a £400 tent, a mosquito net, insect repellents, water purification equipment, or durable, high quality rucksacks and all-weather gear right up to, and including, down-filled jackets and SAS smocks, Survival Aids was the company you turned to. For that matter, it even sold portable global positioning systems which allow intrepid travellers, by means of satellite fixes, to establish their precise location on the planet. By pre-programming such systems, even in the most featureless wilderness, they will literally tell the traveller which way to go.

Although not greatly sports-oriented when he joined the company in 1988, Paul liked the job and quickly took to the outdoor life at weekends, gaining practical experience of the equipment and clothing he was selling. In November, 1989, he was transferred to Glasgow to manage the chain's Buchanan Street shop.

Pauline, who hails from Dundee, had come to Glasgow to undertake a primary teacher training course at Jordanhill College. Having moved into a rented flat, she found herself a job as a part-time sales assistant to augment her small student grant. Fairly quickly, though, she discovered she hated both her course and teaching. In that, she was not unique; teacher-training has one of the highest drop-out rates among students. When eventually she quit college, she decided to stay on in Glasgow. The part-time job in a Buchanan Street shop became a full-time one, and she was to remain there for under a year until the retail outlet closed down. Casting around for another job, she became a sales assistant at the Survival Aid's Buchanan Street outlet, some two years before it went out of business.

A couple of months before the company finally went into liquidation, staff had heard rumours that the chain was in financial difficulty. The problems related principally to its operations south of the border, and the expense of maintaining the costly catalogue service which it ran. In contrast to the rest of the organisation, the turn-over for the Glasgow branch was fairly healthy, running at some £450,000 a year. However, it, too, suffered from some of the company's generic problems: Over-staffing and poor stock rotation.

Based on the trading figures he had already seen, and the weekly through-put of customers, Paul believed that the Buchanan Street shop would still have a future, operating on its own, Quietly he began amassing information on its operations. When the axe fell, he decided to attempt to take over the business. But for that he needed a partner, someone who could join him in raising the necessary start-up capital. He was extremely open about his plans and went through the shop, offering every member of staff the opportunity to join him in a rescue take-over. The only one to take him up on the offer was Pauline, who said she could probably raise £10,000. Paul said he could match that, and the partnership was born.

Pauline says, "Although I hadn't been working terribly long in the shop, I'd seen enough to satisfy me that we could make a go of it. I also enjoyed working there. Besides, when you looked about, there weren't too many other jobs around. I felt that this was an opportunity to do what I wanted to do."

In Pauline's case, it was her parents who were prepared to go guarantor on a £10,000 bank loan. Paul had approached his grandmother, who owned a farm, and in the parlance of Cumbria, was "quite minted."

Even with that backing, raising the necessary finance proved a Herculean task. In fact, putting together the financial package was by far the toughest part of the whole operation. "It was three and a half months between the closure and the new opening. At times it felt like three and a half years," admits Paul. "There were times when I thought to myself, 'You're wasting your time; this is never going to happen.' It was all taking too long. There were just too many problems."

At the outset, immediately after the closure, Paul had got in touch with the liquidator, indicating that he was interested in taking over the shop, and acquiring some of the chain's former stock. That done, the pair's first port of call was the Scottish Enterprise Business Shop in Bothwell Street, which referred them to the Prince's Scottish Youth Business Trust. After interview, the Trust sent them on a six-day business course at Glasgow College of Commerce. There the young entrepreneurs learned the basics in producing a business plan.

With the knowledge acquired from that crash course, they produced their own business plan. Vetted by the Trust, it was based upon achieving a smaller volume of sales than the old shop, because the couple realised their operation would not have behind it the resources of a parent organisation; they also were unsure how much of the previous trade had been generated by the catalogue mail-outs, which were now discontinued.

From a list of accountants, the two selected a firm to help them prepare the final draft of the business plan for presentation to the bank. It was almost to prove their undoing. "That first business plan almost cost us the business," said Paul. "It wasn't any good. The figures didn't tally up. There was no allowance made for Value Added Tax ... The bank was not at all happy about it and referred us to another accountant who did everything very professionally. Even then, the bank people were still a bit iffy about the whole idea."

The caution was understandable. The would-be shop owners were young and relatively inexperienced. And Paul and Pauline, like many a business couple before them, found themselves being waltzed around on a merry-go-round of somewhat reluctant financiers. It was Mark Twain who humorously likened bankers to men who, when the sun was shining, tried to press upon you an umbrella, but at the first sign of rain demanded it back. With that sentiment, Pauline would most heartily concur.

"Basically, you had to prove you could get the money from somewhere else before they would give you it," she said.

Desperate to break the financial deadlock, Paul tried to rope in support from Glasgow Opportunities, an organisation dedicated to helping business within the city. But it wouldn't make a move until the bank authorised a loan of £20,000. In turn, the bank wouldn't authorise the loan without some sort of endorsement from Glasgow Opportunities. Finally it was the Trust which eventually broke the deadlock, advancing the couple a £5000 low interest loan. On the strength of that loan, the bank finally consented to advance the money. The two also qualified for a £40 a week Government business start-up grant for the unemployed - cash which they had already earmarked to go towards the loan interest.

With the finance in place, matters proceeded at a more rapid pace. Through a solicitor, the couple entered into negotiations with the liquidator on a new lease on the property. The deal was a most satisfactory one for the couple. They were given the first three months of occupancy rent-free, and also succeeded in cutting back the original lease from 16 years to five. That was an important victory. In the first flush of enthusiasm, new traders sometimes saddle themselves with over-long leases - forgetting that, if things don't turn out quite as planned, and the business ceases trading, they are still responsible for paying for the remaining years of the lease. As an unlimited company, the young entrepreneurs didn't want to burden themselves with an undue level of risk.

From the liquidator they received a list of unsold stock still available and selected the lines they thought would sell best. As liquidated stock, Paul was able to obtain it at extremely advantageous prices, paying only 40 pence in the £ on its net worth. They got about £16,000 worth of stock from the liquidator, which translated to almost double that amount in real terms. "That was an enormous help," says Paul. "We used that stock in our Opening Sale. Without it, we would certainly have found ourselves paying back people over a much longer time. "

They were not, however, completely reliant on former stock. A lot of Paul's time was spent in contacting other wholesalers and manufacturers, setting up new accounts. Most insisted on money up front, a fairly common practice when doing business with a new company. But others proved more flexible. For a down payment on part of the stock, they were prepared to give 30 days' credit on the remainder. "Obviously we ordered more from the companies who gave us part credit terms, because we could get a lot more stock for our money," said Paul. "Eventually we had £35,000 worth of opening stock which was a pretty good level to achieve."

Most of the stock ordering was left to Paul, because he had a better knack for persuading companies to offer credit terms. However, there were still plenty of other tasks to be completed. The couple had also bought the old shop fittings, but there was a lot of re-organising of the lay-out involved, as well as redecoration, which they carried out themselves. Other vital purchases included some basic tools of the trade - a till; a small, second-hand computer; a £200 fax machine; and a £500 Accept machine for credit card purchases (the machine is hooked up to the card companies' computers, giving an instant playback on cards' credit-worthiness). They also took on three of the previous staff - two full-time and one part-time.

On August 17, 1993, The Outdoor Survival Shop opened for business - to instant success. Their Opening Sale, alone, virtually paid off all their borrowings. By mid-September the shop was in credit, a quite breath-taking achievement.

Paul said: "After the first week of trading, I knew we were going to be OK. A lot of people had been very doubtful if we'd succeed, saying, 'I'll believe it when I see it.' "

Pauline added: "The shop was pretty big to start as a first business, and we were also quite young; perhaps because I'm a girl, I also seemed to get knocked back whenever I phoned a company looking for stock. But the fact is nobody was taking a risk except us - we were the only ones. Actually, the thought of it failing didn't cross my mind. We were always pretty certain the custom was there and we knew the business."

In what is a fairly saturated market - there are some ten outdoor equipment shops in Glasgow - the pair had decided right at the outset that they wanted to keep the same general customer base. "We're quite up-market. We don't do any cheap lines," says Pauline. "We also do a lot of travel equipment which no-one else does. We don't just sell to the public. A lot of people come here for advice. That's where we win. We spend time with customers and tell them about things. That establishes good customer loyalty. We actually hear a lot of horror stories from customers about things which have happened to them elsewhere. All of our staff here have genuine outdoor experience. We wouldn't take on anyone if they hadn't. "

Paul added: "Trying to be as competitive as possible as an independent shop is quite hard. We rely on being knowledgeable on product. Everyone in the shop climbs, walks, skis or has travelled the world. They know what they are talking about."

A measure of that commitment to providing only the correct equipment is the shop's policy on the sale of climbing crampons. It will never sell them to climbers unless they know precisely the make of boots on which they are to be fitted. In fact, often the shop insists on the customer physically bringing in the boots for inspection. Pauline explains: "Some climbing boots are not designed to take crampons. We want to make sure everything is compatible. For our own peace of mind, we would rather have the reputation for doing the right thing, rather than just selling."

In the ever-growing area of outdoor leisure pursuits, the emphasis on safety is a constantly recurring theme. Every year newspapers, often in the wake of some climbing tragedy in the Cairngorms, hammer home the message that the mountains and the severity of Scottish winters are quite unforgiving of mistakes, and that taking the right equipment, in the first instance, is of paramount importance. That undoubtedly increases the level of general public awareness, encouraging people to seek out long-lasting, quality product which will withstand the rigours of outdoor activities - the market The Outdoor Survival Shop wishes to be in.

In the event, retaining a fair slice of the former customer base proved slightly more easy than Paul and Pauline expected. A lot of their former customers simply weren't aware that the shop had changed hands, and continued to roll in. In generating awareness of the company's arrival in the market place to others, Paul says probably the best move was the simple announcement in the shop window that its ownership had changed. Externally, to customers, there may not have appeared to be much to distinguish the new shop from the old - the stock range was similar; even the sales staff faces were familiar. What had changed, though, was the shop's internal administration. It was a much more tightly run outfit. With half the former staff, half the old stock levels, and much improved stock rotation, it began turning in some pretty impressive trading figures. In its first year, The Outdoor Survival Shop easily beat its target of £280,000, achieving a turn-over of £310,000. In the second year, it grossed £321,000 and is currently heading for a target of £330,000, which it expects to surpass without too much difficulty.

Those excellent results did not pass unnoticed. In 1994 the shop won Shell UK Livewire and Kwik-Fit business awards for showing promise, growth and the employment of others. More recently it won a small business award for Glasgow, through a competition sponsored by the

Royal Bank of Scotland. The media publicity those awards engendered also helped promote broader awareness of the company.

In its growth and development, one of the most important measures has been the installation of a £1300 new computer system which now handles all its stockholding and accounts. Prior to its installation, Paul and Pauline had to guess at stock levels, keeping a rough rule of thumb check on how lines were moving. Operating non-computer records was also expensive; their accountants had to physically tabulate all stock movement. Now, with transactions being automatically recorded, the task is a lot simpler - and the accountancy bills correspondingly lower. "We just hand over a floppy disk with all the information in it, which the accountant can copy into his system without having to manually input our records," says Paul.

Having firmly established themselves in their market, the couple are now out to widen their customer base. They have been helped, in some degree, by the continued, and growing, pre-occupation the public has with designer labels.

To increase sales volume, the pair have also started ordering in specialised outdoor equipment, suitable for military use. They run road shows at military barracks, showing off these lines and offering on the night discounts. Soldiers very often buy lines such as SAS smocks in preference to army issue. Recent cutbacks on full-time professional military personnel, however, mean that smaller forces are now becoming better equipped. On the plus side, the shop does a booming trade in selling outdoor lines to Territorial Army reservists.

Glasgow's increasing popularity as a tourist destination has also brought about an upsurge of sales of items such as water bottles to German and Italian visitors setting out to tackle the West Highland Way. However, major growth is likely to come only through the opening of a second shop. It is an option that both favour, and they have been keeping a weather eye open for a suitable city site. However, they are not going to rush into anything. The existing shop services quite a large hinterland beyond Glasgow. Many outdoor enthusiasts travel in from surrounding districts. Any new location will have to satisfy them that it is genuinely bringing in new customers, not merely siphoning off existing ones.

That the market is there is not in doubt. The Outdoor Survival Shop succeeded to a business which, in its final year of trading, was turning over £450,000 worth of stock. Pauline and Paul are still £120,000 adrift of that performance.

As an independent, The Outdoor Survival Shop has demonstrated in classic fashion that small can be beautiful. However, retail - even in a strong niche market - is dependent upon growth of sales volume. The big challenge for the company is undoubtedly to translate its winning formula to another location, with all the attendant cost benefits that ordering for two outlets can bring. If that happens it will be no more than the company is due. Paul and Pauline exhibited considerable faith in getting the business off the ground, overcoming all the hurdles flung at them, through a mixture of tenacity and common sense. They have earned the right to reap the rewards of expansion.